Kevin N. Wright

EFFECTIVE PRISON LEADERSHIP

Kevin N. Wright

EFFECTIVE PRISON LEADERSHIP

Binghamton, New York

William Neil Publishing
4 Lincoln Avenue
Binghamton, NY 13905-4320
(607) 722-5090

Printed in the United States of America

Library of Congress Catalog Number: 94-092257

ISBN 0-9642806-0-4

Second printing 1997

DEDICATED TO
THE MEMORY OF NEIL WRIGHT
An Effective Leader in Education, Criminal
Justice, and His Family

CONTENTS

PREFACE

This book is written under the premise that the actions of prison administrators make a difference in the quality of incarceration. That may appear to be a simple enough assumption. But, if it is true, it seems like one should be able to find a book that describes how prison administrators should do their jobs, what actions they should take, what they should pay attention to, and how they should treat staff and inmates. I did not find such a book in my search of the prison literature, and so I decided to attempt writing one.

I, like most penologists, have spent most of my career studying inmates. My goal has always been to improve the quality of incarceration. I studied how inmates adjust (or fail to adjust) to prison, what programs work and which ones do not, who becomes violent and why, and how the social environment affects inmates. These topics are important in understanding and improving prisons, but it was only recently that I began to realize that the actions of prison officials may be the most important factor in determining the quality of life within prisons.

I did not come to this conclusion directly nor on my own. In 1986, I was fortunate to be selected as a National Fellow of the W.K. Kellogg Foundation. The fellowship allowed me to study outside my area of expertise. Being concerned that my research was not always applied, I set out to learn more about the process by which knowledge is put into practice.

The Kellogg Foundation encourages its fellows to study internationally, so I went to Kenya to observe efforts to stem the highest population growth in the world through family planning. As I met with leaders in international and national planning and assistance organizations, I was impressed by their understanding of the problem and well laid out plans. But, when I went into the field with community health workers and observed them encouraging people to plan their families, I realized that the ultimate outcome of family planning depended on the success of the local outreach workers. It was then that I realized the importance of *leadership*.

After being in Kenya, I continued throughout the rest of the fellowship to study grass roots leadership, in this country and elsewhere. As I learned more about motivating people in these settings, I became increasingly convinced that the practices of local leaders were applicable within more formal organizations, and within the organizations that interested me most: prisons.

One year after completing the Kellogg fellowship, I was fortunate to be selected as a Visiting Fellow by the federal prison system. This opportunity allowed me to observe and interact with prison administrators and to begin to compile a set of impressions about how to run a prison well.

Scope
This book is about the basics. I examine what quality incarceration means—what it looks like and what it feels like. In doing so, I set forth a set of fundamental values that I believe are crucial in providing quality incarceration. It is important for prison employees at all levels to recognize these principles for they define what it is that everyone should be striving to achieve—they define excellence.

I then set out to explore how to get there, in particular, how to lead, motivate, and excite employees to do their jobs well. I take the position that there are a few fundamental values that must be held sacred within the organization. Deviation from those principles simply cannot be tolerated. However, employees need to have a say in how these standards are achieved. Leaders must pay attention to the organization's culture and their role within it. They must build community and commitment and they must develop their people.

This is very much a how-to book. I describe how prison officials should do their jobs, what actions they should take, what they should pay attention to, and how they should treat staff and inmates. Since no two people are alike, it is doubtful that you will agree with absolutely everything I say. But that is fine, provided that your disagreement with me helps you clarify your values about quality incarceration and how to get there. To me, that's what is important—having a vision of excellence and a plan to get there. That may seem self-evident but often administrators get so tied up in the day-to-day operations that the mission and methods to achieve their vision are lost.

The book is organized into three parts. The first section examines what is important in running a prison and how to get staff to pay attention to those issues. It is about building connections between staff and establishing a sense of shared responsibility.

Part Two explores what quality incarceration means from the perspective of how inmates should be treated. I argue for a model of citizenship in which inmates are provided with six fundamental rights—the right to safety, care, personal dignity, work, self-improvement, and a future. In the concluding chapter in this section, I examine how to handle the minority of inmates who are disturbed and severely disruptive and for whom the model of citizenship will not be appropriate.

The final section considers the future and how to effectively move toward it. I examine how to develop a vision of excellence and how to use strategic planning to pursue that vision.

Audience

I believe that the principles of good leadership are applicable in any setting, be it a prison, university, corporation, or hospital. The product or constituency does not matter because all organizations are made up of people who have similar needs, for fulfillment, belonging, and achievement. However, this book is, in particular, about leadership in prisons. The principles may be universal but the examples and applications are particular to prisons.

The primary audience I have envisioned for this book is employees at all levels within prisons. For executives, the book lays out how to run a prison well. For mid-level administrators, the book outlines fundamental principles of leadership. And for line staff and new employees, the book describes a set of fundamental values that are crucial to doing a good job.

The secondary audience I have in mind for this book is college students studying prison administration. It has been my experience that it is difficult for students who have not worked in a prison to discuss and comprehend issues about quality management. Hopefully, this book will provide students with a basic understanding from which those discussions can ensue.

ACKNOWLEDGEMENTS

I want to begin by thanking Donald Powell Wilson, a prison psychologist, who wrote *My Six Convicts*, published in 1951. As a young college student searching for some direction in his life, I stumbled on Mr. Wilson's book. The men he described intrigued me; I did not know people like that. That book led me to a career, which now, 20 years later, has been rewarding, fascinating, and fulfilling.

The Kellogg Foundation afforded me the chance in the middle of my career to step back from my work and learn something new—what a rare and wonderful opportunity. As I described above, my pursuits directed me to rethink my perspective on quality incarceration and to refocus my attention on prison administration.

Twice, the Federal Bureau of Prisons has taken me in for a year as a Visiting Fellow. I was welcomed into the federal prison "family" and given the freedom and resources to carefully scrutinize the operations of a major prison system in the United States. J. Michael Quinlan was director then, and we had numerous conversations about what is important in running a prison system well.

Kathleen M. Hawk, now Director of the Bureau, was then the Assistant Director of Program Review and allowed me to participate as a member of several intensive, week-long program audits headed by regional directors. These occasions gave me first-hand experience in evaluating how well prisons were paying attention to details and how well wardens and senior staff were guiding their personnel.

It was during one of those audits that I met Charles Turnbo, Regional Director for the Bureau's Southwest Region. We spent considerable time discussing effective prison leadership as we drove from one prison to the next, and it was during one of those rides that this book was conceived. I owe Charles for identifying many of the fundamental values for which I have argued in this book.

Many others in the Federal Bureau of Prisons influenced this book and provided information for it. But, I am especially indebted to William (Bo) Saylor, Gerald Gaes, and the rest of the staff in the Office of Research. They were my colleagues, my friends, and my teachers during my two years with the Bureau.

Several people read drafts of this manuscript and provided helpful suggestions for its improvement—Phil Spears, Assistant Regional Director for the Northeast Region, Federal Bureau of Prisons; Samuel Lewis, Director, Arizona Department of Corrections; Linda Biemer, Dean, School of Education and Human Development, Binghamton University; J. Michael Quinlan, former Director, Federal Bureau of Prisons; Margie J. Phelps, Research Coordinator, Kansas Department of Corrections; and Richard Rison, Warden, Federal Medical Center at Carswell, Texas.

Judy Gordon is a wonderful copy editor. She lets my voice remain in my writing but weeds out all those testy little grammatical errors, split infinitives, and misspelled words.

Lastly, I need to thank my wonderful family, Karen, April, and Will, who put up with my physical and mental absences while researching and writing this book, read drafts and provided feedback, and continually challenge me to practice what I preach!

THE AUTHOR

Kevin Wright is Professor of Criminal Justice in the School of Education and Human Development at Binghamton University, State University of New York. Wright received his Ph.D. from the Pennsylvania State University in 1977 after earning B.S. and M.A. degrees from Sam Houston State University in Huntsville, Texas.

The Federal Bureau of Prisons selected Wright as their first Visiting Fellow in the Office of Research in 1989. During his year with the Bureau, Wright studied staff perceptions of the work environments in federal prisons. Wright returned to the Bureau in 1991 to examine the effect of management styles on staff satisfaction. During his two years with the Bureau, Wright also provided leadership training, conducted institution program audits, and acted as facilitator for various workshops.

Wright has conducted research in the D.C. Department of Corrections, New York State Department of Correctional Services, City of New York Department of Probation, New York State Division for Youth, Pennsylvania Department of Corrections, and Philadelphia Family Court. His research has been funded by the Office of Juvenile Justice and Delinquency Prevention, the Bureau of Justice Assistance, the National Institute of Justice, and the U.S. Department of Health and Human Services. He has conducted leadership training for correctional professionals through the National Institute of Corrections.

In 1986, the W. K. Kellogg Foundation awarded Wright a
National Fellowship. During his three years as a Kellogg Fellow,
he studied grassroots leadership while traveling to Kenya, Mexico,
China, Brazil, and Ecuador.

Wright is the author and editor of three books, including the
Great American Crime Myth which was published by Greenwood
Press in 1985. He is also the author of more than 30 articles
published in professional journals and seven book chapters. He
serves on the editorial board of the *Journal of Criminal Justice
Education*.

1

GOVERNING PRISONS

Next to God and my family, the Bureau of
Prisons has my heart.
-- statement made by Federal Bureau of Prisons
supervisor

Prison executives face unprecedented challenges today. Inmate populations continue to soar, while state and federal budgets face severe shortfalls. External scrutiny by the press, the courts, and legislative and executive budget analysts is increasingly intense. In some areas, unions are gaining strength and demanding different working conditions. The work force is changing. More women and minorities are entering prison service which, in itself, is good but creates a new set of organizational circumstances. Technology is advancing, becoming more complex and expensive. With growth, prisons and prison systems necessarily increase in size and bureaucracy. The organization becomes more impersonal, leaving employees feeling anonymous and perhaps even alienated. Chains of command become excessively long, decision-making is slowed, and innovation may be stifled.

Within this morass of internal and external changes, prison executives must somehow attempt to maintain stable, coherent, and predictable institutions, where inmates and staff are relatively safe, conditions are humane, facilities are sanitary, and opportunities for meaningful work are available. The challenge is great. To meet these demands, contemporary prison leaders must be highly motivated to achieve excellence, excited about what they do, passionate about mastery of their craft, and sufficiently energetic to get the job done. Passive acceptance of responsibility will not lead to success. Rather, leaders must create an institutional vision of greatness and commit themselves to its accomplishment. They must give their hearts, not just their minds nor just their time. Prison leaders must commit that element of human character from whence fervor, inspiration, and dedication flow.

These are high sounding words—abstract and lofty. Few people working in prisons would argue with them, but when the Governor is calling, the inmates are threatening a food strike, and the safety supervisor has just informed you that the backup generator is insufficient should the facility experience a total power outage, you hardly have time for such lofty thoughts. Welcome to the world of *prison administration*!

Prison Governance

Only recently have people begun to realize that high-quality management leads to well-run prisons. For decades, universities have run schools of management to prepare individuals for responsibilities in private industry. Universities operated programs in public administration to ready the next generation for executive service in the public sector. However, if one wanted to be a prison administrator, he (until recently there were few women) went to the school of hard knocks, starting off in an entry level position in corrections and working his way up, learning along the way how to run a facility.

People who studied prisons, sociologists for the most part, focused on the culture of prisons, studying it mostly from the inmates' perspectives. These researchers scrutinized the complicated web of social relations that developed among the "society of captives," and examined the inmates' exotic language, code of behavior, and hierarchy of status. Sociologists observed a reciprocal relationship between inmates and staff, such that staff allowed themselves to be "slightly" corrupted, overlooking the minor rule infractions of powerful inmates in return for a trouble-free unit that escaped the scrutiny of supervisors.

Unfortunately, these studies provided prison administrators with little useful information. Administrators seemingly had few options other than observing the inmate culture with no ability for modifying its existence or its effect.[1] Only recently have universities, researchers, and prison systems awakened to the fact that bright, well-trained, and visionary leaders are needed to establish and operate well-run prisons.

Fortunately for administrators, recent research by Useem and his colleague Kimball[2] and by John DiIulio[3] has redirected attention away from prison culture and toward prison governance. This research clearly establishes the fact that the considerable variation in the quality of prisons is largely attributable to the effectiveness of prison managers. Some prisons are safe, clean, and humane. Inmates are provided with opportunities to learn and to gain meaningful work experience. Other prisons, however, are far more disorganized, violent, corrupt, and inhumane.

Based upon his study of prison systems in Texas, Michigan, and California, DiIulio determined that while considerable variation in experience, background, and style exists among successful prison executives, four characteristics are common:

1. They have been in their positions long enough to understand what needs to be done, have mapped out objectives, and have begun to implement them.

2. They do not remain in their offices but are out in their institutions. They are keenly aware of what is going on, involved in the day-to-day operations, and attentive to details.

3. They are self-confident and consciously aware of their influence within and outside the organization.

4. They are highly committed and loyal to their organizations and staff.[4]

Useem and Kimball studied prison riots that occurred between 1971 and 1986 (beginning with Attica and ending with the West Virginia Prison) and, unlike previous analysts, concluded that riots are not dissimilar, random events that could occur in any prison at any time. Instead, riots appear to be symptomatic. Their circumstances may differ, but invariably disorganization is a precipitating condition. According to Useem and Kimball, prior to every riot there was a breakdown in administrative control.

Breakdowns resulted from scandals, escapes, inconsistent and incoherent rules for staff or inmates, fragmentation, instability in the chain of command, weak administration, conflict among staff, public dissent, and disruption of the daily routine.[5]

Studies such as DiIulio's and Useem and Kimball's appear to have occurred just in the nick of time, at a point in correctional history when unprecedented forces for change are bearing down upon prison systems. Still, the understanding of prison governance and effective leadership is in its infancy. Studies thus far point out the importance of effective management but give little insight, other than general directions, as to how to run prisons properly. The purpose of this book, then, is to provide practical and useful information about how to be an effective prison leader.

The book does not have all the answers and may only raise a few questions. Reading it will not transform you into an effective prison executive, but it may help you identify the basic values and activities that will help you be a more effective prison executive. As DiIulio has already observed, successful prison administrators "are not here today, gone tomorrow," but, as with all professionals, acquire their skill over time with practice, observation, experience, and progressive responsibility.[6] It is hoped that this book will provide insight into motivating people effectively, reasons for treating prisoners with dignity and respect, and ways to deal with the weighty problems of running complex correctional facilities.

Successful Prisons

So far I have referred to "successful," "well-run," and "effective" prisons without explicitly describing what such facilities look like, how they operate, and what values they exemplify. In searching the academic literature, one finds surprisingly scant descriptive information about successful prisons. Donald Cressey, eminent criminologist, relates the following account by a prison warden:

> "It is like I say around here. A man is tearing up his cell and has just attacked an officer. So I say, Well, let's go over here to the shelf and get one of these criminology books and find out what we should do. There's nothing there."[7]

And so it goes with the academic literature devoted to correctional administration. Duffee, in his book, *Correctional Management: Change and Control in Correctional Organizations*, discusses in detail correctional reform and the importance of management in that process, but fails to describe an effective prison.[8] *The American Prison: Issues in Research and Policy*, a volume edited by Goodstein and MacKenzie, explicitly recognizes, in a series of articles that explore the predominant issues in prison research today, the increased attention to accountability in correctional administration.[9] Yet, this volume fails to articulate a standard to which that accountability must conform. In perhaps the most popular introductory textbook in corrections, Clear and Cole criticize prison administration, suggesting that it "is dominated by uncreative thinking, ungrounded and idiosyncratic conceptualization, and an unwarranted commitment to traditionalism."[10] Yet, they, too, fail to provide their readers with a perspective of the well-run prison. Even DiIulio, who specifically concerns himself with what constitutes effective prison management, summarily describes a good prison as one that "provides as much order, amenity, and service as possible given the human and financial resources."[11]

Fortunately, while academicians have failed to come to grips with what constitutes success, the people responsible for running prisons have not been so remiss. Norman Carlson, past director of the Federal Bureau of Prisons, like DiIulio, was fond of three-word phrases to summarize what he saw as symbols of well-run facilities:

- a good prison stresses care, custody, and control;
- good prisons are safe, clean, and humane; and
- effective prison staff are characterized by pride, professionalism, and proficiency.

During his 18-year tenure as Director, Carlson stressed strict administrative controls and tight discipline, while simultaneously promoting the provision of basic amenities (including good food and sanitary living conditions) and life enhancing programs. Because Carlson believed "imprisonment itself is punishment," he intended his prisons to be safe, civilized, and humane. Under Carlson's regime, prisons sparkled, the food was excellent, inmates worked productively, and the facilities were well-controlled with no shouting or aggressive horseplay.[12]

J. Michael Quinlan, who followed Carlson as Director of the Federal Bureau of Prisons, described a standard for well-run prisons:

> Society should expect that prisons will protect public safety. It should expect that inmates will be confined safely and humanely. It should expect prisons to provide inmates with a reasonable diversity of programs and services that will give them the opportunity to better themselves before returning to the community. It should expect that such programs will be cost-efficient; in practical terms, this means stratifying programs according to inmates' needs (such as educational deficiencies), motivations to change, and severity of criminal history.[13]

When one enters a facility for the first time, it does not take long to determine the quality of management. An unused mop leaning against the wall in the entry way lets you know that the institution lacks administrative attention to detail. From there, you may note substandard conditions of sanitation—dirt and grime in the corners of rooms, cockroaches scampering beneath kitchen equipment, and leaky sewage pipes. Hallways may be dank and dark, with walls in need of painting and floors not recently shined. In poorly run prisons, inmates mill around with no particular destination or work to do. You hear shouts, insults, and incessant testing of one another. Violence occurs routinely and inmates easily acquire drugs and alcohol. Low-quality management produces depressed staff morale and low job-satisfaction. Professional pride among the staff and hope among the inmates rarely develops in poorly run prisons.

I have toured facilities that have such conditions. One is tempted to accuse the CEO's of such prisons of neglect, irresponsibility, and perhaps even dereliction of duty. But, in my experience, these administrators have *not* stopped caring. Instead, what I have observed were weary, overwhelmed, exasperated, and sometimes inept managers. They blamed the legislature, the central administration, the courts, labor unions, and their subordinates for the conditions of their prisons. They felt overworked and unappreciated.

Somewhere in their tour of duty, these managers lost their ability to respond effectively to the significant problems of running good prisons. For some individuals, the key event may have been the constant resistance of inmates, but, more likely, the difficulty of operating in complex public bureaucracies destroyed their ability to visualize and effect change. As a consequence, these individuals lost their enthusiasm, confused their mission, and felt inundated with the day-to-day operation of their facilities. They became bureaucratically impotent.

Prison administrators who find themselves in this position have generally replaced the goal of producing safe, humane, and productive institutions with the goal of keeping the lid on the facility. Their days are so filled with meetings that they seldom have time to reflect on where the organization is or where they want it to go. Problems abound and they jump from one crisis to the next. Seldom are new ideas or new directions proposed. Instead, protection of the status quo and stability are sought. Rather than measuring what has been accomplished, "success" is documented by the number of inmates processed, budget-making and personnel practices, and public relations activities.

These executives view their own abilities as constrained by the layers of bureaucracy above and below them. They feel that budgetary and policy constraints allow few options for change, and they have little confidence in the ability of subordinates to carry out reforms. Because these executives have failed to visualize a course of direction for their institutions, they fall back on policies, procedures, and rules for decision-making. They become preoccupied with administrative requirements, which may blind them to the original goals of running safe, humane, and productive prisons. Merton labeled the problem, "trained incapacity"[14]; Cohen called it the "demonics of bureaucracy." [15] The result is executives who are "functional bureaucrats"[16] rather than effective leaders.

Leadership Styles

Prisons may be one of the most difficult organizations to run. On one hand, stability and control are essential. Any form of disorganization may lead to an administrative breakdown that results in violence or a disturbance. This requirement dictates that prisons be run with strict administrative controls and tight discipline. However, change inevitably presses on all organizations, and, as I have already discussed, the pressure for change is now particularly strong with regard to the operation of prisons. Prison administrators and their institutions must adapt to these pressures. In doing so, administrators run the risk of creating instability, disorganization, disruption, and conflict.

It is indeed a frightening situation. John Gardner, past Secretary of Health, Education, and Welfare and advisor to six presidents of the United States, claims that the vitality within contemporary organizations rests upon the willingness of men and women *throughout* the institution to perform as leaders, by identifying problems and working to solve them. Without such action, organizations become unimaginative, sluggish, and rigid bureaucracies that are unable to adapt to a swiftly changing environment.[17]

During the 1980s, Japan took the lead as an industrial giant in the international market, while the United States declined steadily in its ability to function in technological, financial, and manufacturing spheres. This decline sent analysts searching for explanations of Japan's superior performance. The answers have been fairly consistent: American organizations, both private and public, are sluggish and self-serving, while Japanese organizations are vibrant and customer-oriented. Quality performance and a passion for excellence distinguish Japanese performance.

The efficiency-oriented management style of American organizations distances managers from workers and depersonalizes their relationships. Managers think, plan, and guide subordinates who are thought to be less able. Rules and regulations, which tend to be inflexible and unresponsive to change, are used to maintain organizational control.[18]

The quality approach differs significantly. Quality is everyone's *responsibility*, not just management's. Everyone is expected to take *initiative* to ensure high quality performance. People are organized into teams that understand their roles in producing the whole. People and units work in concert. Regular, timely feedback is provided. Knowledgeable staff, spread throughout the organization, take the initiative to pinpoint problems and develop ways of solving them.

Prison executives can begin to develop quality-oriented organizations by:

- demonstrating their own commitment to the approach by shifting their goal from personal achievement to quality performance;
- providing training, education, and a climate that supports experimentation and change;
- trusting staff to take responsibility for their own actions;
- listening in order to establish a partnership with staff in problem solving;
- sharing the management tasks;
- being responsible to inmates, staff, and the community by devotion to service; and
- institutionalizing feedback about performance that is used to correct, not punish.[19]

The pursuit of quality requires fundamental transformation in the way most prisons operate and the way prison executives perceive their own jobs and responsibilities, their opinions about their staff, and the manner in which rewards and punishments are distributed. Initiative and responsibility must be shared throughout the organization.

Not everyone working in corrections will agree with what I have just said. My critics contend that the work of managing prisons is too tempestuous and dangerous to allow such flexibility. They argue for a paramilitary, hierarchical administrative structure that concentrates authority at the top of the organization and maintains a downward articulation of superior-subordinate relationships. Formal rules, regulations, procedures, and policies govern staff behavior and leave little discretion to the individual. Centralizing function and control routinizes activities, limits uncertainty, and increases predictability.[20] In prisons structured hierarchically, people know their roles and their responsibilities. Little is left to chance. Everything is by the book. Decision-making tends to be uniform and consistent.

Highly structured organizations require autocratic managers, absolute rulers who hold and exercise power unilaterally. Through their control, these leaders assure clarity, order, consistency, and efficiency. They constantly audit, police, and enforce policy. Adherence to procedure is rewarded, while dereliction of duty or independent action is punished. In this manner, autocratic leaders set high standards of discipline. They guarantee that rules are coherently articulated and consistently applied, that conflict does not surface, and that lapses in security do not occur.

The problems with autocracy are twofold. While successfully promoting continuity, autocracy tends to be excessively rigid, disavowing change and alienating employees in the long run. Prisons once resided in relative seclusion, located in rural areas, and, unless a riot took place, received little attention from the public, the press, or government officials. Now, prisons dwell within complex and turbulent environments and experience persistent internal and external pressures for change. Administrators can no longer seek only continuity, but must instill non-disruptive, continual adaptation to the forces of change within the organization.

The need for change creates an administrative tightrope for the executive to walk. Prison executives cannot successfully run prisons alone; they need the support, commitment, and contributions of their staff to sustain the vitality of the organization. Bold men and women may challenge systems, charismatic individuals may lead organizations through troubled times, but the day-to-day success of an organization depends upon ordinary people performing their duties well.[21] High performance within prisons depends on the behavior of the line staff. Line staff must be motivated to achieve excellence and feel responsible for what happens in the institution. For this to occur, staff must be involved and share in the leadership task. If their people are not expected to use their decision-making abilities, then they will assume, and reasonably so, that they are not responsible for what goes on within the institution. Autocratic leadership stifles initiative, reduces responsibility, and leads to feelings of anonymity, powerlessness, and alienation.

I want to be perfectly clear about what I am advocating. I am not promoting the democratic management styles that were popular in the 1970s, for they tended to absolve everyone of accountability. Organizations need leaders who are responsible for the mission and activities of the organization. Followers need leaders because they desire, even expect, decisiveness in times of crisis and want someone to take care of the day-to-day operational decisions of running the organization. Full participation in everyday decision-making would bog the organization down in trivia. But people like to be consulted, to have their say about important issues that directly affect their lives, and to have opportunities to solve problems and try new ways of doing things. Broadening participation in decision-making produces more pluralistic organizational governance, but does not exonerate leaders from being leaders. The proper and primary role of leadership should be to foster a sense of ownership in the organizational mission among staff and to enable them to do their jobs with a high degree of commitment and responsibility.

Effective prison leaders balance the need for continuity with the need for change, and the need for standardization with the need for self-expression and creativity. Effective prison leaders view their staff as mutually interdependent, and they constantly work to ensure a sense of community among them. At times, that involves unswerving dedication to tradition—operation of safe, humane, and productive prisons—but it also requires adaptation of custom to accommodate new conditions.

Judgment

The men and women who analyze and write about leadership these days, both in private and public sectors, tend to be focusing on the social side of the enterprise; that is, how to motivate and organize people. However, an important characteristic of leadership, not inherently social yet imperative for prison executives, is sound *judgment*.

It is important to recognize that good judgment is not synonymous with intelligence. People who exercise good judgment have good mental capacity, but intelligence does not guarantee good judgment. Judgment involves the ability to combine facts, information, and intuition to assess situations and make realistic decisions about how to respond.[22] A good judge is part analyst, part fortune teller. Judgment involves speculation about the future and anticipation of probable outcomes.

I was once part of a group of civilian men and women being taken on a tour of a maximum security facility by an assistant warden. This individual was a brilliant program developer, but his opinions often conflicted with those of individuals responsible for custody. On the day of our tour, the assistant warden decided to lead us through the dining hall during the noon meal. The catcalls and uproar from the inmates grew steadily as we passed through the room. The supervising lieutenant glared at the assistant warden as he led us out of the dining room and muttered under his breath, "asshole."

This executive exercised poor judgment. He failed to consider the ramifications of his actions. In the operation of prisons, such mistakes can be momentous. Change and disruption tend to reverberate throughout the organization. Eventual outcomes must be anticipated, and when change must be undertaken, contingency plans must be carefully constructed.

PART ONE

RUNNING A TIGHT (BUT LOOSE) SHIP

In his famous study of America's best-run companies, which led to the publication of *In Search of Excellence*, Tom Peters found that top corporations are both centralized and decentralized. They are fanatical about a few centrally defined values but push autonomy down to the shop floor to encourage commitment, innovation, and personal growth. The underlying structural forms of these organizations are neither traditionally bureaucratic nor the more recently advocated democratic form. Instead, they are lean on the top with cohesive teams at the production level. Leadership in these companies is highly hands-on and value driven; chief executives regularly visit their stores and plants and evaluate them on the values that the corporation holds dear.[1]

Prisons should be similarly organized. Central administration, whether at the correctional system level or within a particular institution, should take an active, hands-on role in seeing that a few fundamental values (security, humaneness, and productivity) are stressed. Attention to the detail of seeing these values realized should be their fundamental duty.

The actual realization of these values occurs at the line staff level. Every staff member should feel responsible for ensuring institution security and cleanliness, attending to the health and self-development needs of inmates, and making sure that inmates are involved in productive activities. These functions are overlapping and interdependent. Because they are the root source of quality, line staff must have the necessary autonomy, information, and lines of communication to ensure their achievement.

The five chapters of this section discuss how prison executives can strive toward the delicate balance of running tight but flexible organizations. Chapter 2 begins with a list of details for running effective prisons. Chapter 3 revisits the topic of quality prisons and explores how executives can pursue quality with all the fiscal and regulatory constraints imposed on contemporary prison administrators. Chapters 4 and 5 address ways to push autonomy downward within the organization and ways to develop people, give them responsibility, and trust them. These actions are necessary to achieve a high degree of commitment, to avoid alienation, and to build teamwork. Finally, Chapter 6 discusses how to put these ideas into practice and presents a perspective of leadership which will make it possible.

2

PAYING ATTENTION TO DETAIL

Staff and inmates will do what you inspect,
not what you expect.
-- Charles Turnbo, Regional Director and Former
Warden, Federal Bureau of Prisons

Pursuit of quality in prison administration requires dogged attention to detail. By detail, I mean making sure that the institution meets or exceeds predetermined high standards of operation. This requires that executives know what they want their facilities to look like. Tom Peters found America's best-run corporations to be excellent on the basics. These companies focus on quality, and work hard to keep operations simple and concentrated on this one issue.[1] Prisons should be no different.

During his tenure as Director of the Federal Bureau of Prisons, Norman Carlson focused on the basics. As mentioned in Chapter 1, Carlson liked to summarize what he considered important in running prisons. He wanted clean, safe, and humane prisons, and he earnestly pursued them. He continually inspected his prisons to assure that they met his standards.

The practice of frequently inspecting prisons to ensure the quality of care and custody is not a new convention. When John Howard, father of the penitentiary, became sheriff of Bedfordshire, England in 1773, he exercised the often neglected custom of touring local prisons. The conditions shocked him; the prisons were overcrowded, lacked discipline, and were devoid of sanitary conditions. Thousands of prisoners died each year from disease. In his book, *The State of Prisons in England and Wales* (1777), Howard outlined a standard for operating institutions in which prisoners should be "properly lodged—fed—clothed—instructed—worked." He argued for "the utmost regularity, order and cleanliness" and stated that there should be "no drunkenness, no riot, no excessive misery, no irons, no starvation."[2]

Setting Standards

If the overarching goal is a safe, humane, and productive prison, then one must have an idea of what standards of safety, humanity, and productivity he or she aspires to achieve. These standards must be realistic. Over time, as staff make improvements, standards may be elevated. If a facility has no industry, it may be unrealistic to expect initially to have all inmates engaged in some meaningful activity throughout the day. Perhaps, the work of maintaining the facility and participation in programs combined occupies inmates for four hours each day. In this case, then, the standard to diligently audit is that all able-bodied inmates engage in at least four hours of daily activity. The goal for the facility may be to increase productive activities available to inmates from four to six hours per day.

After an institution sets a standard, then it must be someone's responsibility to see that expectations are met. The more global a standard is, the more people will be needed to share responsibility for it. Safety, for example, must be the responsibility of everyone employed in the facility. Staff must understand that being responsible involves more than simply being accountable. Responsibility carries with it *commitment* to achieving the standard. This requires that staff not only attend to the condition in the moment, but that they take initiative to inform others of problems, suggest improvements, and work toward raising the standard. Diligence and constancy characterize the pursuit of quality.

To assure the maintenance of standards and the resolution of problems, it may be necessary to assign someone the duty of inspecting conditions and taking corrective action. It is reasonable, even imperative, to expect all prison employees to attend to key control, but in the day-to-day activities of operating the institution, who inspects the fire extinguishers to see that adequate pressurization is maintained? Many prisons resolve this issue of responsibility by having a safety inspector, who, among other things, maintains all fire extinguishers.

One prison that I visited introduced a new program to emphasize its ongoing, but routine, quest for high standards of sanitation. Procedures to assure cleanliness and safety had been written for each unit within the institution. Every unit and all employees were expected to meet these standards. In making their rounds throughout the facility, administrators regularly checked institutional conditions. But, to that which becomes routine, it is often difficult to be vigilant. So the facility initiated a "white glove" program. Each quarter, the safety inspector toured the facility literally wearing white gloves. He checked cleanliness as well as other conditions and prepared a written report of the results of his inspection. This program heightened attention throughout the institution to the importance of sanitation. It created a challenge and reinforced sanitation as everyone's responsibility.

Fundamental Elements of Quality

What then are the *basics* for a well-run institution? They vary somewhat, depending on the prison system, the level of security, and the regional location of the facility. So far in this book, three fundamental attributes have been stressed: safety, humaneness, and productivity. These characteristics should be sacred in operating every institution; however, they may be too broad to guide specific practice as prison executives begin to stress attention to details.

Warden Ron Burkhart at the Federal Correctional Institution in Fort Worth, Texas, developed the following list of 15 essential elements for effective leadership and management which are comprehensive, action oriented, and would assure that a facility would be safe, humane, and productive. While the list may not exhaust the possibilities of important details, prisons that achieved a high quality of performance in all 15 areas would indeed be judged as well-run.

Sanitation

High standards of sanitation establish a symbol for inmates, staff, and visitors of a commitment to humane treatment and a pattern of excellent care. They set a touchstone of civility for the entire prison.

A facility should have a comprehensive plan which attends to sanitation, health, and beautification of the facility. The plan should be ongoing, not merely situational. Each unit should contribute to the overall plan by establishing its own plan. Staff and inmates should be involved in the development and implementation of the plan and should be encouraged, not to simply satisfy expectations of routine inspections, but to take pride in the overall conditions of the facility.

Inmate Programs

The orderly management of a prison depends upon effective programs for the inmate population. Programs that motivate, are well-organized, and are at the interest and ability level of inmates support a climate of concern, productivity, and growth. They allow inmates to find meaning in their incarceration. Programs also give inmates hope and something to work toward, which tends to heighten commitment to acceptable forms of behavior within the prison. Consequently, involved and active inmates generally pose fewer security problems.

Security

Security is the responsibility of all staff and must be attended to with vigilance. Training is essential so that staff clearly understand all policies and procedures. Regular communication is needed to remind staff of existing standards and to inform them of any changes. All employees must be on the lookout for irregularities and must feel they have a duty to communicate those problems to the appropriate individuals. Corrective action must be taken immediately. Security is an inter- and intra-departmental responsibility; communication must flow horizontally, as well as vertically.

Key Control

The security of an institution depends on effective key control; its compromise may pose a threat to the safety of inmates, staff, and the general public. Staff should be continually reminded of the importance of key control in department meetings. Problems must be reported immediately. Accountability must be carefully monitored and duplication of keys must be controlled.

Tool Control

Tool control is equally important to the overall security of the prison. Effective control prevents use of tools as weapons and in escape attempts. But, tool control procedures also assist in over-all institutional operations by improving the appearance of shop areas, keeping equipment in good repair, maintaining inventories, and teaching proper work habits to inmates. Compliance with storage and inventory procedures can be assured by careful inspections and auditing as well as continuing education of staff.

Visibility

Visibility of staff throughout the institution helps deter significant problems. Prison staff stay apprised of activities within the institution and develop a more complete image of the operation of the facility. Staff can respond to concerns, deficiencies, and problems before they escalate to crises. Staff presence sends out several messages to the inmate population: that staff are interested, available, and responsive and that they are maintaining constant surveillance of the facility. Their circulation throughout the facility fosters more complete communication and networking among staff and inmates.

Communications

Communication serves as the *lifeblood* of any organization and is especially critical in a prison. Through constant and effective communication with inmates, staff stay informed and can react to problems before they escalate. Staff keep one another informed of what is happening within the institution through discussions and feedback. Members within a well-functioning prison communicate freely with one another without fear of reprisal. This means that staff, rather than hiding mistakes and problems, face them so corrective action can be taken. Because communication is so crucial in the prison setting, information must be conveyed accurately and in a professional manner. Training to improve written and verbal communication skills should be an ongoing process.

Responsiveness

Attention to detail demands unequivocal observance of policy, procedures, and individual requests. Logs must be completed and monthly reports written on time. Inmate requests, phone calls, and requests for information from the public, the press, and members of the legislature must be answered in a professional and timely manner. It may be necessary to prioritize the order of response, but *all* requests deserve serious replies.

Staff Training

Training serves as the key to the development of a professional prison staff. Training is not simply something that happens when an employee joins the organization but is an ongoing process of development. It must be an institutional priority which is programmed into the life of the organization. Departments and individuals need yearly training plans that are consistent with the prison's mission and the individuals' career goals.

Inmate Accountability

The institution should have clearly articulated policies for acceptable inmate behavior which should be carefully explained to each new arrival. At all times during the day, inmates should have assigned areas and activities. With this system established, inmates should be held accountable for their actions and whereabouts. Individuals who are late for work details or programs should be appropriately counseled and disciplined. Active participation and contribution in the performance of job duties and program involvement should be expected. Inmate misconduct should not be tolerated and rules should be swiftly and consistently enforced. It is crucial that all prison staff, regardless of position, be part of the inmate accountability system.

Staff Accountability

Staff also have duties to which they must be held accountable. They must perform their jobs as specified by policy and be responsible for the quality and timeliness of their performance. High standards of expectation, mutually developed by the supervisor and staff member, will generally result in a higher quality of performance. A component of staff accountability includes preventing and exposing corruption. Prisons and their executives must be vigilant in their investigations of employee involvement in inmate abuse, improper relationships, theft, and trafficking in contraband.

It is also critical that supervisors be held accountable for holding their people accountable. For example, some correctional officers do not write good disciplinary reports; the description is so poorly written or lacks sufficient detail that a good case cannot be made. Good supervisors kick back poorly written reports to be redone. Not-so-good supervisors pass the reports on to the disciplinary administrator, who then has to dismiss the case. The supervisor may then sympathize with the officer, thereby giving the impression of "standing behind his men," when in fact neither the officer or the supervisor have been held accountable for their performance.[3]

Teamwork

Individual compliance with policy and procedures and subscription to high standards of professionalism alone will not produce a well-run prison. Much of the work of operating institutions involves common tasks—security, caring for the emotional health of inmates, scheduling, and programming. Teamwork (intra- and inter-departmental) is crucial. Staff throughout the facility must appreciate their mutual interdependence and realize that by pooling their talents, energies, and resources, they will be more effective. Effective communication and mutual respect are essential to the development and maintenance of teamwork. Equally important, inevitable conflicts must be allowed to surface so they may be addressed.

Professionalism

Professional practice incorporates the character, spirit, and methods of sound and appropriate prison operations. On one hand, professionalism demands individual integrity, loyalty to the organization, honor, and trust. It includes attention to attire, mannerisms, and appropriate communications, as well as conscientious policy compliance and performance of one's duties. Professional practice symbolizes a commitment of staff and the institution as a whole to a set of fundamental principles of humane and appropriate actions. It allows prison employees to lead by example.

Policy Knowledge and Compliance

The rule-of-law establishes that power be exercised within a set of explicitly and coherently stated regulations. Governance by the rule-of-law avoids capriciousness, uncertainty, and misunderstanding. Thorough and clearly articulated policy serves as the cornerstone of a system of rule-of-law within an organization. For that system to be effectively implemented, universal knowledge of policy and constant monitoring of compliance are essential.

Completed Staff Work

Prisons are complex organizations composed of individuals performing numerous interrelated tasks. Often the culmination of a larger project depends on the punctual completion of specific activities or tasks by individual staff members. For the prison to operate smoothly as a well-integrated system, staff must complete all work in a timely, organized, and professional manner. The effects of unfinished work generally reverberate throughout the organization. Constant attention to quality is essential, for a job worth doing is worth doing right.[4]

Paying Attention

If one accepts these as the fundamental values to assure quality imprisonment, then the next step is to consider how to pay attention to them. In other words, how does an executive make certain that staff attend to these details? At the risk of being redundant, there appear to be *three* key components in assuring quality control in administration of prisons: policy, proficiency, and pride.

Policy specifies a particular course of action that has been determined to be expedient and effective within the organization. In their entirety, policies serve as the rules of governance for a prison. They clarify for both staff and inmates the parameters of acceptable behavior and the consequences of rule infraction. Policy serves to constrain behavior and increase predictability. It reduces capriciousness and individual discretion, thereby enhancing uniformity and equity of treatment.

By formalizing rules of behavior, sanctions, and procedures, policies transform organizations into mini-governments.[5] They form the constitution, the laws, and the legal system of the organization. As such, they explicitly stipulate how power should be exercised within a well-defined set of constraints.

Within a prison, governance by policy ensures accountability. Inmates are expected to act correctly. Rules of conduct are specified and clearly communicated. The consequences of misbehavior are carefully spelled out. The same is true for staff. Each group may hold the other accountable for its actions. The more thorough and complete a set of policies is, the less likely it is that fragmentation will exist, misunderstandings will occur, power will be abused, and disorganization will arise.

You may be wondering how an organization that relies heavily on policy written to constrain behavior can maintain the flexibility that I argue is essential. The rule-of-law is concerned with the proper exercise of power. It holds power accountable and governs its use; nothing more, nothing less. Policy codifies those constraints and makes governance coherent and predictable. Beyond that objective, policy has little role. In explicit detail, it sets the *minimum* standards of acceptable behavior and practice, but must stop there and allow staff the autonomy to accomplish the goals of incarceration.

Policy should be carefully written and frequently reviewed. It should form a living charter for the organization which is used daily and not left to gather dust on the shelf. Policy compliance and knowledge should be frequent topics for training and continuing education of staff.

A second, but related, ingredient for assuring attention to detail is *proficiency*. Adeptness, capability, competence, expertise, and mastery denote proficiency. Proficient prison workers comprehend their duties and ably perform them, they know prison policy and appreciate its importance in administering a correctional facility, and they recognize the seriousness of imprisonment and perform their jobs responsibly.

Being proficient demands recognition of the three elements of professionalism: character, spirit, and methods. Beyond simply knowing how to do one's job, proficiency encompasses the commitment and enthusiasm to do the job well and the integrity to be honest and straightforward while doing so. The concept of mastery seems particularly important. To master one's job requires an individual to be in control. With experience comes a natural tendency to be relaxed and careless in the performance of duties. This tendency negates the value of experience. Mastery, therefore, includes both skill and discipline.

A final key element to maintaining attention to detail is *pride*. My father-in-law, who helped me renovate a turn-of-the-century home, often reminded me that "a job worth doing, is worth doing right." When I begin to do something in a hurried and haphazard fashion around the house or in my work, just wanting to get the job done, his words slip into my consciousness. If I am going to expend my energies, I might as well do the job so it will make me feel *proud* of my efforts. When assimilated into one's personal philosophy, this simple message becomes a powerful self-motivator to achieve high standards of performance. At an individual level, pride implies self-respect and a sense of dignity. It contributes to self-esteem but also requires self-esteem.

At an organizational level, pride demands attention to detail. The institution must look right, smell right, and work right. Group pride tends to include a spirit that reinforces and builds upon itself. Small gains contribute to the desire to make more progress, which leads to a natural momentum within the organization toward excellence.

In the prison business, attention to detail—to minute, everyday particulars—is an excellent place to build cohesion and a sense of group responsibility for the operation of the facility. Getting

everyone committed to seeing that details are taken care of—
feeling bad when they are not and good when they are—is what
organizational pride is all about. Quality demands fervor, energy,
and passion.

Organizations often set goals and doggedly pursue them until
they are accomplished, only to turn around, set a new set of goals
and begin again; never pausing to savor and reflect upon their
accomplishments. Leaders can contribute to the development of
pride by celebrating achievement. Taking time to publicly recognize and acclaim what the organization has accomplished will
make people feel good and give them a sense of sharing and
camaraderie.

Integrity

Several studies have been conducted to determine the
characteristics that followers most admire in leaders. The first
choice of preferred personal traits has been amazingly consistent
from study to study: people want honest leaders![6] They want the
people who direct, guide, and make major decisions that affect
their lives to be trustworthy, ethical, and principled. Leaders who
fail to follow through with agreements, make false promises to,
deceive, and undermine their staff quickly lose the allegiance,
loyalty, and support of their people. Staff may work together
without trust but cannot coalesce into a team without it.

One of the quickest ways of losing trust is through hypocrisy.
Followers quickly recognize the sham of leaders who advocate
excellence, quality, and taking care of details, but abdicate those
virtues in the performance of their own responsibilities. Leaders
must model the way.

They must behave morally and ethically. Minor violations of
ethical policy—accepting a bottle of whiskey from a vendor at
Christmas, taking pens and pencils home to their school-age
children, or having their secretaries take care of their personal
business—do not go unnoticed. Being a flirt or a philanderer
compromises a leader's integrity, as does excessive drinking.[7]
Never forget the symbolic role of leadership. Leaders have a moral
obligation to set a high standard of ethical practice.

Being visible and present within the institution is an important component of integrity. It indicates to staff that a leader cares enough to check things out personally, to make sure standards are being met and that the needs of staff and inmates are being fulfilled. Leaders use their knowledge of what is going on in the organization and act upon it in an even-handed manner.

Integrity rests upon consistency. When staff know what their leader stands for, they do not have to wrestle with uncertainty and try to outwit some hidden agenda and political game. Knowing the values of the leader avoids confusion, indecision, and conflict. When rules are uniformly applied and no one receives impunity, integrity avoids inequity. Integrity instills within the organization an elemental commitment to inviolable human values.

It is interesting how the fundamental essence and character of an organization depends, from the start, on the integrity of its leaders and gets defined by actions so simple as consistency, practicing what you preach, commitment, and caring. The nice thing about the simplicity of integrity is that it is easy to begin modeling the way. Starting today, get out into the institution and never again walk past a compromised detail (whether it involves security, sanitation, or staff or inmate amenities) without commenting and taking action. As a leader, your response should be corrective, your responsibility is to support the effort, and your reaction should be punitive only as a last resort.

Go overboard on attention to ethical and legal standards. Inspect everything, root out corruption and impropriety. A law enforcement agency cannot stand for any breach of lawfulness; it undermines the integrity of the entire organization. How else can you demand appropriate behavior of inmates and justify their punishment to them?

Abolish all unwarranted and petty rules and procedures. Policy should reflect what is preeminently important to the organization. Any proscription beyond that point will limit adaptability and can be used to control staff behavior beyond the point where necessary. Staff know when rules are "Mickey Mouse" and are being used to fulfill some manager's need for power.[8]

It all boils down to being genuine as a leader. The organization's purpose and advancement have to be your primary focus. As a leader, you must be unfailing and dependable in your commitment to the organization and its people, you must be determined and resolute in making the place better, and you have to pay attention to the little things that make people feel good about themselves and make the organization more successful.[9]

3

CREATING QUALITY PRISONS

Occasionally, I am asked to conduct management assessments of prisons. These audits typically require that I spend several days at a facility observing its activities and procedures and interviewing personnel so that I can prepare a written report evaluating the management of the institution and suggest ways to improve its operations. These evaluations are always stressful for the CEO and executive staff for they are ultimately responsible for the conditions of the institution and the morale of the staff and inmates. Any deficiencies detected—compromises of security or sanitation, low staff satisfaction, fragmentation, or inmate unrest—reflect on the ability of the executive team to properly administer the institution.

These audits often begin with an initial meeting with the warden, the executive staff, and all department heads so that everyone knows what is going on and scheduling can occur. I vividly recall the opening remarks of one warden; he told his staff that his 5-year old son had awakened him at 2 a.m. that morning, that when he went down to the kitchen at 5 a.m. he found that the dog had "crapped" all over the floor; now, along with the auditing team being there, he had a dentist appointment at the close of the day. The warden's words were honest and unpretentious. He admitted that it was a stressful time for him and that he would be glad when the week was over. It would seem that such sincerity and unassuming style would be desirable traits in a chief executive, but several staff mentioned to me during the week that they did not know whether the warden really cared about what happened in the prison. For you see, leaders can rarely afford the indulgence of speaking for themselves, for their actions and words both formal and informal serve as symbols for the entire organization. Leaders set the tenor for the organization; they reflect its mood, set its course, and define its vision.

In opening the meeting by associating the program audit with being awakened in the middle of the night, having to clean up the dog's mess, and going to the dentist, the warden casts a negative image on the entire evaluation. The message could have been very different had he begun the meeting by saying that he was pleased to have the auditors there because the staff had done some important things of which he was particularly proud. He could have then gone around the room and recognized the efforts of department heads who exemplified the initiative and behavior he desired of all of his managers. This approach would have focused attention on the organization rather than the CEO, portrayed the audit as an opportunity rather than a burden, highlighted pride rather than obligation, recognized high performing staff, and helped clarify for staff and visitors the warden's values. That's how you serve as a symbol!

At a similar staff meeting to review a management assessment report that I had written, we began late because the director of the system had just returned from touring a particularly overcrowded prison with a senior legislator. The CEO opened the meeting with myself and his executive staff by recounting some of his conversation with the legislator, telling us how he had set the representative straight about conditions of the facility by telling him that, "yes, the conditions are atrocious, unsanitary, and dangerous, but it is out of my hands. He told the legislator that the system had dutifully taken all convicted offenders sent to it by the courts and continued packing them into an already overcrowded facility, and that he lacked funding to improve services or for building additional space. The CEO's message was an important one to communicate to the legislator, but the manner in which he retold it to the staff conveyed an underlying theme that the staff was "off the hook" regarding the conditions of the prison.

A saying that I find to be particularly applicable to prison administration is that when you are up to your armpits in alligators, it's hard to remember that your original objective was to drain the swamp. As I listened to this last executive, it became apparent that he had succumbed to the alligators. With his opening remarks, he abdicated himself and his staff from responsibility for the problem. The message to his staff was that he understood that they were in this together, that he knew they cared, but that he recognized they were fighting a losing battle. His words conveyed a sense of hopelessness.

One act of self-revelation or blaming external forces by an executive will not send an organization spiraling into apathy. Yet, the regular voicing of even subtle messages that change and achievement are impossible, that success will be elusive, and that the organization and its people cannot make a difference or have a positive influence on prisoners, will have a serious impact on the organization's social climate. Worse yet, leaders can give the impression that they do not care about staff, inmates, safety, sanitation, or whatever. Certainly, the group or issue rendered inconsequential and unimportant by the actions of the leader will not be attended to with any regularity, precision, or care.

Culture

Leaders give meaning to the activities of an institution through their words, their actions, and, importantly, their reactions. Leaders define what is important and what is unimportant, what is possible and what is impossible. Creating and maintaining a basic philosophy and set of values are essential acts of leadership. Research has shown that effective organizations may differ greatly in their fundamental values, but they all share three common qualities: (1) *clarity* about what the organization stands for, (2) *consensus* among members about those values, and (3) *intensity* about the importance of the values.[1]

The basic philosophy, expectations, and norms of an institution compose its culture. Cultures tend to be enduring, evolving from the interaction of history and mission over time. The culture of a "Big House" such as Statesville differs from that of a low-security camp such as Allenwood. Many factors contribute to the culture, including identity, tradition, openness, staff turnover, diversity, and cohesion.

The response to significant incidents—assaults, suicide attempts, fires, and disturbances—portrays an important part of the culture of most penitentiaries. Fellow officers convey esteem on the most ardent staff in responding to these events. New staff are socialized into the ethic of responsiveness and must prove their mettle. Storytelling, the recounting of significant incidents, helps maintain the culture by reaffirming the value of responsiveness. In this way, the culture of the prison is purposeful, it gives meaning to the organizational identity and defines what is important.[2]

All prisons have cultures. Some are positive and others are dysfunctional. Stressing the basics—safety, sanitation, and productivity—is an integral part of the cultures of high-performing prisons. Typically, one finds *clarity*, *consensus*, and a fairly high level of *intensity* regarding these values in high-performing institutions. On the other hand, staff in poorly run facilities tell stories about the biggest rat they've seen, they dehumanize inmates in their stories, and they recant examples of when the administration failed to stand behind staff. Informal rules regarding acceptable levels of graft, corruption, and dereliction of duty exist within these cultures.

Recognizing and paying attention to prison culture is essential for an executive. Cultures resist change but can be moved. Executives fortunate enough to inherit prisons with positive and vibrant cultures must be cognizant of the need to renew the culture to avoid stagnation and fragmentation. Less fortunate executives face the task of overcoming the inertia of institutionalized poor performance, internal conflict, lack of enthusiasm and commitment, disorder, and rigidity. Recognizing the importance of language, of the stories told, the symbols, and the drama that occurs constitutes the first step in transforming the institution's self-image.

Unfortunately, law enforcement personnel often develop a *we/they* sense—"*We* must stick together because *they* are against us." The "they" are the criminals who resist the staffs' efforts to help, as well as attempts to control, them; the politicians who neither understand nor care about what law enforcement personnel are up against; the courts who side with the criminals; and the public which does not appreciate what law enforcement does for them.

Having so many antagonists provides law enforcement personnel with many targets for blame. "We cannot do that because of the _____."

Exceptional leaders overcome the tendency to blame others and create an inspiring institutional purpose. James McGregor Burns calls this "transforming leadership" and claims that it results when leaders "arouse, engage, and satisfy the motives of followers." According to McGregor, transforming leadership arises when a person engages others to perform at higher than ordinary levels of motivation and morality. They may start off with different purposes but are drawn together to work for a common objective. Various adjectives have been used to describe such leadership: inspiring, exhilarating, energizing, and uplifting. McGregor claims that transforming leadership is inherently *moral* in that it elevates the human behavior and, importantly, the ethical purpose of the leader and followers.[3]

Transforming leaders give meaning to an institutional vision. They set standards of *quality*. They lead by example and serve as symbols. For their staff, they:

- promote a strong sense of personal achievement,
- encourage and inspire loyalty,
- foster agreement about organizational objectives,
- expect moral and ethical behavior,
- promote commitment to hard work and caring for one another,
- diminish job stress and tension.[4]

From spending years studying successful leaders, Tom Peters and his colleague, Nancy Austin, claims to have "learned nothing about magic. We've learned, instead, of passion, care, intensity, consistency, attention, drama, and of the implicit and explicit use of symbols."[5]

Attention

In the previous chapter, I argued that achieving quality and excellence depends on attention to detail; the message in this chapter is that people are going to pay *attention* to you because you are the leader. What you say; how you say it; your body language; with whom you speak; how you spend your time; where you go in the institution (or whether you go); and who gets promoted, rewarded, or reprimanded, are all significant within the organizational culture. They serve as symbols and create the *drama* of the organization.

"What I do can't possibly make that much difference," you might respond. Warren Bennis notes in his book, *The Unconscious Conspiracy: Why Leaders Can't Lead*, that one study found that when school teachers had high expectations of their students, that alone contributed to a 25-point increase in students' I.Q. scores![6]

What were the fundamental values of the Jimmy Carter presidency? Human rights was one, and ...—it is difficult to recall anything beyond that single issue. With Ronald Reagan, who can forget: lower taxes, stronger military, less government. Regardless of whether Reagan accomplished any of these things and irrespective of your political ideology, you knew where he stood.

What gets attended to, gets done. If you desire quality, then focus on quality. That's it, plain and simple. Getting started may feel awkward. You may not know what to say, or how to be explicit about what you want, but it doesn't matter. Your people will get the message. Staff pay attention to what the boss wants. What's important is for you to initiate the message.[7]

Attention to details includes monitoring what you say and how you spend your time in order to uncover the true messages your words and actions convey. One way to begin is to assess what you do. Analyze your calendar for the past week. How did you spend your time? With whom did you meet? What were the topics of the meetings? Next, pull out your memorandum file and see what you have taken the time to communicate in writing to the staff over the past month. What do these correspondences indicate about your priorities? What was their tone? Complimentary? Critical? Discouraging? Inspiring? Next, examine your correspondence file to determine what messages you have been sending people outside the institution. Finally, analyze your phone log. Who have you been talking to and about what? Now then, ask yourself what messages you have been sending. Will your words and actions move, motivate, and incite others in the direction you want the organization to go? If not, change your routine!

The 4 C's of Quality Prison Management

After reading this far, you may be left with the impression that successful prison executives must be half drama coach and half cheerleader. Attending to the drama of the organization and encouraging and cheering others along serve as important activities for successful executives. But, neither a *rah rah* spirit nor a charismatic personality are required. Running prisons is serious business. Being *serious* about quality and about how to achieve it, stating the message simply, meaningfully, and establishing it as part of the institutional culture, are imperative.

As elementary as this task may appear, it is actually quite difficult to achieve. Most prisons are overcrowded, under-budgeted, thinly staffed, and occupied by people who take pleasure in disrupting institutional operations. One can easily slip into a reactive mode, running from one crisis to the next, never pausing to consider where the institution is headed.

George Camp, in his study of prison crowding, identified four attributes of leaders who successfully manage crowded prisons: *candor*, *caring*, *commitment*, and *confidence*.[8] These four characteristics also apply to sound prison management in general.

Candor

Synonyms of candor include directness, forthrightness, frankness, honesty, and sincerity. People appreciate leaders who tell it like it is, do not play political games, do not hold back, and are thoroughly honest and genuine in their actions and words. Candor informs followers about where they stand and apprises them of the whole situation. From that, followers possess the elements of predictability and can go on with their work and their lives.

In the past, universities have withheld statistics about graduation and campus crime rates from prospective students; hospitals have not told terminally ill patients that they are dying; the military has covered up dishonorable actions during conflict; and schools have denied students honest assessments of their achievement by passing them on to the next grade. This lack of forthrightness has consistently undermined the integrity of these institutions. When a young student is raped in her dormitory, an investigative reporter discovers that not a single member of the basketball team has graduated in the past five years, the atrocities of war are revealed, or some student graduates who cannot read or write, the image of the institution suffers.

Whether the issue is the potential for promotion, the danger involved in a particular assignment, the chances for additional resources, or the priority of a particular project, you may be able to nudge employees along, but when they find out that you have not been open and straightforward, you will lose their allegiance.

Often the most difficult times to be candid are the times you truly care about the persons with whom you are dealing. You do not want to hurt their feeling or disappoint them, so you withhold information. When the truth surfaces, your genuine concern will be undermined by your lack of candor.

Caring

It is highly improbable that a prison executive who does not sincerely care about the welfare of staff and inmates will successfully create a safe and humane environment. In the case of inmates, irrespective of their past acts or their present behavior, prison workers must hold a fundamental belief that all people deserve humane treatment. Otherwise, what motivation exists to treat inmates well? If one does not believe inmates have basic human rights and deserve individual dignity, then how inmates are treated is irrelevant. The conditions of incarceration, the squalor of the housing units, and staff abuse do not matter. To produce a quality product, one must accept that the customers—both inmates and the public—deserve high quality services.

It is equally important for prison executives to be genuinely concerned about the well-being of staff. If followers perceive that leaders do not care about them, they will be alienated and lack commitment to the mission of the institution. A study of fired corporate executives found that they were arrogant, aloof, and individualistic, and they preferred to work independently. They were often excessively critical of their staff. Fired executives viewed participation and discussion as a waste of time, frequently made insensitive or untactful remarks, and viewed staff with considerable mistrust.[9]

Caring about both staff and inmates involves:

- treating them with respect,
- treating them with dignity, and
- treating them as adults.

A big step in demonstrating care is to get to know people, spend time with them and learn what's troubling them. That requires that executives get out into the facility, and that they stop and talk to staff and inmates. It helps to learn peoples' names and something about them. Receptivity is equally important, giving the impression of openness and the desire to hear what they have to say.

To be sensitive, one has to actively listen, not simply stand quietly and let the person speak, but to hear and respond appropriately. This does not mean that executives have to acquiesce to complaints, demands, or suggestions, nor should they undermine the chain of command. But, everyone deserves a response: "no, the policy is...;" "I don't know but I will find out;" "you need to talk to your counselor about that;" "I will look into that and get back to you;" "I am glad you told me that; I will take care of it;" and so on.

Commitment

The people of the United States tend to define their identities by what they commit to, whether it is their religion, the kid's soccer team, their family, their work, or their hobbies. Americans are joiners. They get involved in professional organizations, civic associations, social and service clubs, and recreational programs.[10] It is easy to recognize the executive who's burned out, nearing retirement, or no longer dedicated to the job; he's committed to his new motor home; that's what he talks about, and what he thinks about. Good leaders belong to several organizations—some civic, others service, and hopefully at least one that is recreational. But most importantly, good prison executives are involved and committed to their own institution and build meaning into their own lives by their commitment. Why do they commit themselves? Because they believe in the values and the mission of the organization.

The quickest way to find out if you are committed to the institution is to consider your priorities. Have you written them down? Discussed them with your staff? Next, ask yourself if you respect what you do. Are you loyal to the institution?

Confidence
Lastly, leaders must believe in their ability to make a difference. If leaders give into the alligators, then the game is over. The opposite of confidence is pessimism, and if leaders feel helpless then one can be fairly certain that the followers will feel incapable. Lack of confidence implies the loss of hope and allows images of failure to creep into individual and organizational self-images.

John Gardner argues for "tough minded optimism," which joins hopefulness with realistic assessment. Life is a challenge and poses a steady stream of problems for people. Fortunately, in the long process of evolutionary adaptation, humans acquired the ability to respond to challenges.[11] In fact, people may be at their best when struggling. George Orwell wrote in his novel, *The Road to Wigan Pier*, "that many of the qualities we admire in human beings can only function in opposition to some kind of disaster, pain or difficulty."[12]

But optimism must be tempered with realism, otherwise you look foolish; like Pollyanna, you will be regarded as someone who dreams unrealistically. When times are tough, budgets are being slashed, the population of the facility is bulging at the seams, staff are fatigued, angry, and frustrated, and the inmates are restless, it is difficult to stay committed or to remain focused on enhancing the operations of the prison and to truly believe that you can make a difference. That's where "tough minded optimism" needs to kick in.

Emotion
Some readers may have noticed that emotional words keep creeping into my discussions of high-performance leadership and

the pursuit of quality. Words like "passion," "intensity," "caring," and "commitment." Prison executives tend to be a hard-nosed, rational, no-nonsense lot. Emotion doesn't fit into their tough-minded, pragmatic orientation. For some, it may seem like fluff; for others it may be incompatible with their strong, self-reliant image of themselves; and, still others may view emotion as inappropriate to the prison's strict environment. But, emotion drives an individual or a group toward excellence.

Max DePree, CEO of Herman Miller, a leading furniture manufacturer and a company named by *Fortune* magazine as one of the best places to work in the United States, uses an even more provocative word to characterize the emotional state of high performance: *"Intimacy!"* Depree claims that intimacy is the soul of competence. It involves understanding, believing, and practice. One must be intimate with one's work.[13]

For a leader, there are internal and external dimensions to intimacy. Internally, one must possess that special feel and sense of competence that comes with practice. A sense of control and mastery allows one to experience ownership of the activity. Externally, leaders achieve intimacy with their people when they enable rather than encumber them. They provide a sense of focus, continuity, and momentum.

False intimacy is betrayed by superficiality. You have encountered individuals who have the trappings of effective leadership. They are bright, ambitious, energetic, and well-educated. Yet, they fail because they never become responsibly involved in their work. They remain safely detached, aloof, and dispassionate, and everyone knows it.[14]

4

DEVELOPING PEOPLE

Don't choke initiative with policy.
-- Charles Turnbo, Regional Director and Former
Warden, Federal Bureau of Prisons

Throughout this book, I have argued that the pursuit of quality, whether in running prisons or something else, requires that leaders run tight, but loose ships. Tight, in the sense that the organization and its leaders recognize and articulate a set of values that define what the organization is about and then earnestly and persistently pursue those deeply held beliefs. But, loose in the sense that the institution functions as a relatively independent problem-solving organization where autonomy for getting the job done is pushed downward within the institution.

Control

New executives occasionally have the opportunity to hire a few key personnel when they assume their duties, but they seldom experience the luxury of hand picking their entire staff. Consequently, leaders are generally stuck with the followers they inherit. Some staff may be exceptionally proficient and dependable; others may not be as competent. The influx of new, inexperienced staff that accompanied the growth in incarceration added to this problem for many prison administrators. One wonders whether rookie staff and new managers can be trusted to do their jobs well. Do they have sufficient knowledge to carry out their duties?

Do they possess the core values of the institution? Can one depend on them in times of crisis?

Appreciating the critical nature of prison administration and recognizing that their reputations are on the line, many executives focus on the necessity of paying attention to details and seek ways of ensuring accountability and limiting uncertainty. A common response is to retain as much authority, power, and decision-making responsibility as possible. Out of a desire to prevent mistakes and ensure predictability, some executives insist on highly structured organizations that centralize control to hold prisons on course and to achieve quality incarceration. They perceive their job to be making definitive decisions, issuing orders, and carefully monitoring how subordinates carry out those commands. Advocates of this notion believe that top managers can control everything—the mission, personnel, inmates, money, and resources—and thereby can guide the institution in a desired direction.

According to one author, the proper role for correctional officers should not be that of a professional but rather that of a bureaucrat, just as soldiers are bureaucrats. Correctional staff, except at the highest levels, should act according to a few simple operational rules. By routinizing operations, highly bureaucratic prisons minimize the use of arbitrary power and unequal treatment of inmates. They limit uncertainty and increase predictability.[1]

Ironically, the structures intended to assure quality control often produce exactly the opposite effect. A study of professionalism among prison staff found that a commitment to a professional identity (e.g., a belief in self-regulation, a sense of calling to the field, a belief in public service, and a view of the organization as a major referent) lowers role conflict, work alienation, and isolation. In particular, the research discovered that a belief in self-regulation is the most important dimension effecting the three outcomes. Staff dissatisfaction may be reduced by allowing prison workers greater, rather than less, control in decision-making and the discharge of their responsibilities.[2]

For 16 hours each day, the men and women employed in prisons function as adults. Most employees effectively raise their children. They manage complex family budgets, borrowing money from financial institutions that trust them, and make sound investment decisions. They repay their loans and establish good credit. They maintain homes, deciding when to put on a new roof and finding the best deal for the most reasonable fee. Prison employees coach Little League teams, organize softball tournaments, and serve on decision-making boards of churches and other non-profit organizations. Most of them act responsibly, fulfill their obligations, and live moral and law abiding lives.

Sadly, during the eight hours they work each day, prison employees in many institutions are treated as children. They are not trusted, and they know it! Control and decision-making are centralized because prison executives believe that employees cannot be relied upon to perform their duties, to be responsible, and to make the right decisions. Managers assume that employees are lazy, careless, unreliable, and dishonest. Even if executives do not intend to convey this message, it comes through poignantly in a centralized structure. Treat people as undependable, and they will start acting that way.

Unfortunately, more often than not, traditional organizational structures and managerial methods leave people feeling alienated, isolated, and uncommitted.[3] Study after study has demonstrated that the more an organization tries to control its employees, the less likely it becomes that individuals will excel.[4]

To evaluate the quality of performance of an institution from a traditional perspective, one needs only to examine the caliber of decisions made by a few central executives. However, outstanding leadership is evidenced more in the behavior of followers than in the activities of the leaders.[5] One must look beyond institutional executives to see how the people charged with actually carrying out its activities—maintaining safety, teaching inmates, issuing clean laundry, assuring that the housing units are tidy, repairing vehicles—are doing. Are they motivated? Are they reaching their potential? Are they deeply committed to the institution? Are they developing into promising leaders themselves? The art of leadership involves freeing people to do their jobs in the most efficient and competent way possible.[6]

People attracted to traditional methods assume that external factors motivate people, that people work for pay, promotion, and prestige. From this perspective, workers must be offered inducements to perform desired tasks, and managers monitor the workers' behavior to assure compliance. The traditional bureaucratic perspective assumes that people avoid assuming personal responsibility for their actions. Centralized control, highly structured lines of authority, and strict discipline guarantee adequate performance.

An alternative belief asserts that people are motivated more by something within them: pride, self-esteem, dignity, and a sense of involvement and belonging. Contrary to the traditional view, the alternative perspective views people as seekers of meaning, for whom service and contribution to others are equal, if not more powerful, motivators than external rewards.[7] More than 50 years ago, the Hawthorne studies discovered that considerations other than economic and physical design factors affected productivity.[8] Since then, research within organizations has consistently shown the importance of social factors in worker satisfaction and motivation.[9]

Psychologists, Edward Lawler III and Patricia Renwick asked readers of *Psychology Today* what factors were most important to them in a job. The top six responses, ranked in order of importance, were:

1. the opportunity to accomplish something that made them feel good about themselves,
2. the chance to do something worthwhile,
3. the chance to learn something new,
4. the occasion to improve skills,
5. the autonomy to do their job,
6. the freedom to do things that they do best.

Out of 18 items, respondents ranked salary 12th.[10]

People need two things from their organizations. They like to feel part of something, that they belong, and that others respect their contribution. Secondly, people need autonomy to feel as though they have some say, some control of their own destiny within the organization.

Researchers at the University of Michigan's Institute for Social Research conducted an extensive study of organizational control, collecting data from public and private sectors, and found that increased involvement in decision-making contributed to greater organizational effectiveness and higher job satisfaction.[11] Research conducted in private-sector businesses found that decision-making participation increases commitment and profitability.[12] Corporations have experimented with various methods to increase involvement, including quality circles in which workers regularly meet to solve problems, employee stock ownership programs, and self-management work teams.[13]

So you see, the internal motivations are there, waiting to be released. People want to excel, to be high performing, to accomplish something worthwhile. But more often than not, the big, impersonal bureaucracies in which they work leave them feeling alienated, resentful, and powerless.

Ownership

Prisons experience high rates of turnover among employees, averaging 16 percent nationwide and reaching over 40 percent in some settings. Various reasons have been advanced for this phenomenon—the stress associated with prison employment, the unpleasantness of working with inmates, the lack of prestige, and low pay—however, when researchers from the Arizona State University studied why prison staff terminated their employment, they found that departing employees gave none of the usual explanations. Dissatisfied staff cited two reasons for leaving: *the quality of the work environment and lack of opportunities to influence institutional policy*. Neither the lack of safety nor the difficulty in working with inmates led people to quit. Instead, lack of variety, autonomy, authority, and learning opportunities predicted turnover. Prison employees wanted some control and influence in their daily activities—they wanted to be challenged and to have the opportunity to grow professionally. Furthermore, they wanted some say about policy decisions.[14]

In my own research conducted while serving as a visiting fellow at the Federal Bureau of Prisons, I found in responses by more than 3,000 staff to questions about the social climate in federal prisons that individuals with greater input into decisions expressed higher overall satisfaction with their jobs, their facilities, and the Bureau. They also believed themselves to be more effective in doing their jobs.[15] Research conducted elsewhere linked input into decision-making with lower levels of job-related stress among prison workers.[16]

Private enterprise has found their employees to be more productive, committed, and satisfied when they have some decision-making say. Companies which use an assembly line have long been plagued by quality control problems because workers lack commitment to the final product. When General Motors and Toyota entered into a joint venture and opened the New United Motors Manufacturing plant in Fremont, California, they installed a "pull rope" on the assembly line. When workers detect a quality problem or fall behind, they pull the cord and stop the entire line. This simple modification empowered workers throughout the line to pay attention to quality and provided them with a method to respond to problems. This plant has one of the best quality records in the American auto industry.[17]

Whether they manufacture automobiles or supervise inmates, the issue for workers is one of *ownership*. Is the product theirs or some executive's? Are they personally responsible for the product or is responsibility vested with the top echelon? From the workers' perspective, if the ownership of the product rests with someone else, then concern for quality must also be someone else's responsibility. People who "own" their job and "own" their organization feel strong, capable, and committed.[18]

The prescription for building a feeling of ownership among followers is fairly simple. Rosabeth Moss Kanter outlines four steps:

1. Allow people to work on important issues.

2. Trust their judgment and provide them with the freedom to do their jobs.

3. Give praise and recognition.

4. Build relationships for your people, connecting them to sources of power and resources and to opportunities to learn and develop.[19]

An ancient Chinese proverb aptly expresses what organizational researchers are now discovering:

If you want one year of prosperity, grow grain.

If you want ten years of prosperity, grow trees.
If you want one hundred years of prosperity, grow people.[20]

In other words, your greatest legacy as a leader may be how you develop your people to carry on after you are gone.[21]

Delegation

Organizational psychologists, Edwin Hollander and Lynn Offermann, suggest that true staff development must go beyond expanding the influence of staff (sharing power) to providing opportunities for staff to have autonomous decision-making responsibility (distributing power). For this purpose, Hollander and Offermann find that *delegation* may offer a better method than undirected participation. Delegation is not indiscriminate in the allocation of responsibility and power; rather leaders consider the ability, time, and position of followers in allocating decision-making tasks. In this manner, power is distributed selectively rather than equally.[22]

People clearly like to be consulted, to have their say about important issues that directly affect their lives, and to have opportunities to solve problems and try new ways of doing things. But, people often desire, even expect, decisiveness from their leaders. For many of the day-to-day decisions, which way a decision goes does not really matter; someone simply has to decide. Someone has to marshal things along, divide up the tasks, and follow up on progress. In times of crisis, quick, unequivocal decisions are absolutely necessary.[23]

The promise of participation can also unduly boost expectations among followers that all of their suggestions and ideas will be incorporated into institutional operations. When leaders fail to routinely accept their suggestions, followers may come to feel that participation is a sham. Furthermore, some leaders may lack skills to manage group processes and conflict. Significant institutional costs may be associated with requiring these individuals to foster participation.[24]

Leaders must lead. They retain responsibility for their segment of the organization, but, whenever appropriate, they should involve others in the operations of the institution by delegating power and autonomy to make decisions. Perhaps Tom Peters best articulated the appropriate act of leadership:

> Leaders exercise 'control' by means of a worthy and inspiring vision of what might be arrived at jointly with their people; and understand that empowering people by expanding their authority rather than standardizing them by shrinking their authority is the only course to sustained relevance and vitality.[25]

Sharing Power

Getting started as a leader who enables others involves considering the power one possesses as a result of being in a position of authority. One perspective of power views it as "power over" others; with position comes the authority to define the job to be done and the responsibility to see that it gets done. To ensure a high rate of compliance and predictability, persons in positions of authority use power to direct and control the behavior of subordinates. From this perspective, power is a fixed quantity. "If I give you some of my power, I will have less."

An alternative perspective sees power as "power to" rather than "power over." Viewing power from this perspective requires a fundamental adjustment to one's thinking, for power is regarded as energy, potential, and competence. The more people within an organization feel they have power and can accomplish something, the greater their sense of ownership and commitment to the organization will be. They feel vested in the institution. From this perspective, power is viewed not as a limited quantity, but as an expandable one.[26]

To strengthen followers, to help them find in what areas they can be their best, and to support their discovery of their strengths and weaknesses, one must distribute power by transferring authority, responsibility, and, most importantly, initiative. Let others be creative and put their energies and talents to work.

By enabling others to grow and develop, leaders form the basis for reciprocal relationships, based upon mutual trust and confidence. Under these circumstances, followers are more likely to feel respect and commitment toward their leaders and to be willing to make extraordinary efforts. In essence, by strengthening others' influence, leaders, in turn, strengthen their own influence. As team members begin to feel like family, share values, and feel a sense of personal stake in the operations of the institution, then the potential for unique and remarkable levels of performance exists. As the team rises above the individual interests of its members, it starts to function as a cohesive, collaborative, and supportive working unit that relies on cooperation rather than competition, openness rather than secrecy, and strength rather than weakness.

Functioning in this role, leaders add two methods to their repertoire: that of *catalyst* and that of *facilitator*. Acting as catalysts, leaders recognize that people have a stake in what happens in the organization and that they will, if given the chance, try to effect a positive outcome. Catalysts help people exercise their creativity and imagination. They provide the spark by encouraging their people to discover what they can be at their best.

Once that spark is ignited, the predominant activity of leaders should not be control (giving orders and monitoring behavior) but rather facilitation. Leaders should constantly ask themselves what resources, knowledge, and technology others require to proceed and where those necessities can be obtained. Leaders facilitate by removing barriers, resolving conflicts, and building relationships and networks. Facilitators find sponsors and mentors to support the endeavors of others.

Exactly how do leaders do this? Although not an exhaustive list, a few possibilities include:

- However difficult it may be, ignore the limitations, faults, and inadequacies and focus on the strengths, positive attributes, and skills of others. Help them discover at what tasks they can perform their best. Focus on gains, not losses; on opportunities, not problems; and create winners, not losers.
- Encourage others to be creative, to be innovative problem solvers, to take risks. Reward successes rather than punish failures.
- Seek a shared vision for the institution by finding common ground, encouraging collaboration, and planning as a team.

- Build a climate of trust by sharing information, giving visibility to the efforts of others and having confidence in them, and being open and forthcoming.
- Support the efforts of others by providing resources, technologies, knowledge; removing barriers; establishing networks; and resolving conflicts.[27]

Focusing on the positive and creating a climate of trust involves maintaining a delicate balance in the business of running prisons where errors can be costly. Circumstances arise when mistakes, omissions, and overt acts cannot be ignored, and critical feedback is necessary. A manager would be remiss to ignore them; however, leaders must consider how they deliver feedback.

Prison administrators commonly respond to mistakes and omissions by punishing the wrongdoer in hopes of deterring the employee at fault as well as others from making the same mistake. Yet, punishment alienates the recipient and chips away at the climate of trust. Alternatively, leaders may avoid personalizing the issue by not emphasizing blame. Rather, they recognize the problem and work with the staff member in resolving the current situation and avoiding it in the future. The focus in this case, rather than punitive, is corrective. Leaders still get their message across, but the individual responsible for the problem learns that the executive supports his or her efforts, is concerned with quality (not unbridled compliance), and is sincere about teamwork. Leadership is exercised by example rather than control.

Structure

So far, this chapter has maintained that leaders can best strengthen their people by delegating responsibility, sharing power, and fostering ownership. Changing the institution structurally by pushing decision-making downward will help empower employees. Traditional prison bureaucracies have been organized in a pyramid fashion with distinct divisions of labor, stronger vertical than horizontal lines of communication, and power and information concentrated at the top of the pyramid. As we have noted, this organizational structure alienates people— leaves them feeling powerless and without a sense of ownership.

Traditional bureaucracies produce inefficient communication processes: one function may not consistently receive reliable information from another functional area; information acquired at the line level of the organization may flow upward slowly; and information needed by the line staff and known at the highest levels of the organization may be withheld, delayed, or distorted in its downward flow.

Experience within private- and public-sector organizations has shown that formation of small, self-managed teams within the organization avoids many of the alienating effects associated with large bureaucracies and increases productivity and job satisfaction.[28] Self-managed teams are vested with control over both the management and implementation of group tasks.[29] In prisons, the practice of unit management exemplifies this form of organizational structuring. The federal prison system began experimenting with unit management in the early 1960s and has since adopted the practice at all facilities.[30] Since then, many states have also employed these self-managed teams.

Unit management improves institutional administration by directly incorporating the principles discussed in this chapter. Under unit management, the inmate population is divided into smaller, more manageable groups and a multidisciplinary staff is permanently assigned to these units. Units consist of small, self-contained living sections for approximately 50 to 120 inmates. Staff have administrative authority for all aspects of the inmates' daily living and programming. Within the Federal system, the unit staff includes a unit manager, case managers, correctional counselors, a full- or part-time psychologist, and a clerk-typist. Staff offices are located within the inmate housing module and are open approximately 12 hours each day, 7 days per week.

Unit management increases institutional and inmate control by vesting authority and decision-making powers with those staff most closely associated with inmates. Increased and repeated interaction builds continuity into staff/inmate relations and provides for better communication and understanding. Information collected about inmates from interactions and observations becomes cumulative and thereby provides a much richer source of knowledge about inmate behavior. Staff understand inmates better, know what to expect, and can anticipate problems before they reach critical proportions. Dealing with the same staff allows inmates to learn what to expect from staff, what staff expect from them, and where the limits are.[30]

The frequency and intensity of contacts between staff and inmates also contributes to more positive programming. Because staff get to know inmates better, classification and program planning can be more individualized. Adjustments in living arrangements or programs can be made easier. Also, the multidisciplinary expertise of the unit staff enhances the quality of assessments and program planning. Unit management provides for program flexibility by offering specialized services at the unit level (intensive alcohol counseling, for example) that do not have to be provided to the entire population.

Some top executives may feel uneasy about giving up control of these functions. They may wonder whether they can depend on line staff to make critical decisions. Yet, most prisons are too large for a few administrators to get to know all the inmates well. Unit management provides for more efficient and informed decision-making because the individuals making decisions spend the most time with inmates.

Unit management also serves an important staff development function. Through increased involvement in correctional processes and decision-making, unit staff gain valuable experience in correctional management. The practice allows senior-level administrators the opportunity to observe and evaluate the performance of unit staff in making decisions and using discretion. This opportunity helps identify potential leaders early and allows administrators to develop the leadership skills of staff.

Providing unit staff with a sense of autonomy fosters feelings of ownership. It suggests that executives trust their staff. Control of inmates becomes the unit's (rather than solely management's) responsibility. A well-functioning unit staff acts as a team, cooperating and building cohesiveness. Team members are proud of their work and committed to quality. But good teams do not occur automatically. Leaders must facilitate the development of high-performing teams. Chapter 5 describes some things leaders can do to develop teamwork and communication.

5

CREATING COMMUNITY, BUILDING TEAMWORK, AND ACTING LIKE FAMILY

So you see, this is what you get from lousy Government bureaucrats, most of whom make less than $30,000 a year—loyalty to each other, selflessness in the line of duty, and dedication to protect the public they serve.
-- former hostage, Atlanta and Oakdale riots

The Federal Bureau of Prisons refers to the phenomenon as "family." John Gardner labels it "community." Some people call it teamwork. But when a group of people coalesce to pursue some commonly agreed upon objective, an important transformation takes place within an organization. One often observes this occurrence during times of crisis—when a tornado hits the community or a riot breaks out in a prison. During these potentially tragic situations, the shared purpose and the necessity of working together become very clear. People give selflessly of themselves, work long hours in adverse conditions, and sometimes even risk their own lives to save another. In these situations, people show how deeply they care for one another. And during these times, one often observes extraordinary levels of performance.

Such transformations do not occur only during crises. From time to time, they develop as part of everyday work within an organization. But, whether you call it community, family, or teamwork, the phenomenon involves fusion, the bonding of people in a common purpose. Whatever separate interests people hold, whatever individual goals they possess, they achieve social cohesion and bond themselves together in the pursuit of a common goal. Their interaction is mutually supportive. They realize that their own success depends on that of others. They encourage and support one another. They share power, risk, and accountability. Wherever you find community, you observe unity, trust, and a willingness to put the welfare of the group first. You find a climate of pride. In forsaking self-interest, team members rise to a higher level of motivation, morality, and performance.

Characteristics of Cohesion

Pathological families exist where emotional and physical abuse commonly occur and members seldom express love to one another. Likewise, organizations can deteriorate from a group that shares a sense of purpose into numerous self-interested cliques rift with conflict and animosity. Members, even those with outstanding individual abilities, can become so wrapped up in their own self-worth and advancement that they never perform effectively within a group. However, I am using the words family, community, and teams to refer to healthy, vibrant, and uplifting social organizations of people.

If you have worked in corrections for a long time, you have probably encountered prisons where the staff has become splintered into competing factions, between unions and management, custody and treatment, or just groups that no longer get along. You may have come across facilities which lack coherent administrative direction so that everyone makes up the rules to go by. You may have observed prisons with considerable fragmentation, conflict, and instability. Such prisons generally have more discipline problems, higher rates of violence, and lower job satisfaction and greater turnover among staff. They tend to be ripe for disturbances. These facilities have lost their sense of community and family, and their ability to work as teams.

Social cohesion and commitment to a common set of values characterize well-functioning prisons. Members share an obligation and responsibility to one another. Effective prisons have in common the following six characteristics of community:

Connectedness, Caring, and Trust

A vital aspect of any social organization is some level of benevolence, in which personal connectedness binds people together. In its most fundamental manifestation, people working in prisons care about the physical welfare of one another. They protect each other, occasionally placing themselves at considerable risk to save a fellow worker. Altruism explains part of the motivation behind these acts of self-sacrifice, but self-interest also plays a role. I count on you to protect me; in return, I am willing to protect you.

With prison work, concern for one another's physical well-being is a near universal value; however, beyond this fundamental level, considerable variability in the need to be connected exists. Where one finds community, one also observes a recognition of the benefit of being connected. Employees vest themselves in relationships with fellow workers, and the relationship in itself has value to them. Here again, altruism plays a role in promoting general connectedness, but self-interest is important.

In the "community" workplace, people recognize that their success depends on the successes of others, that working cooperatively produces mutual benefit and shared rewards. They expect to receive and give assistance and know that they can depend on one another. Operating in an atmosphere of trust and reciprocity, they can be open and forthcoming, disclosing their intentions, offering ideas and resources, and requesting assistance. Interactions based upon mutually beneficial exchange result in relationships characterized by friendship, cohesion, and positive morale.[1]

A prison setting that lacks a sense of community tends to be ruled by the effects of individuals acting in their own self-interests. Staff define their success in terms of their ability to control, gain authority, and move up the ladder. In these settings, competition dominates. Competitors view the successes of others as threatening, with the aggregate effect supporting a strategic, cautious, and indirect way of relating. Not trusting one another's intentions, staff offer assistance reluctantly and may even sabotage each other's efforts. Manipulation is commonly practiced in settings lacking community. Such interactions often result in hostility, distrust, and low productivity.

Energy

To gain an initial impression of a prison's social climate, I ask staff how they felt when they awoke in the morning. If they tell me they had trouble getting up, that they were tired or sluggish, and, in the worst case, that they dreaded coming to work, I can be reasonably sure that there is a problem. Alternatively, if staff tell me that they slept well, that they had no problem getting up, and, in the best case, that they were excited to get to work, then I usually find the prison to have a healthy social climate. It has been my experience that workload, the number of hours worked, and the intensity of the work have less to do with fatigue than does how well people within the organization get along. Where staff share a sense of commitment and work together congenially, they feel good about their jobs and about coming to work. When the work environment is rife with tension, conflict, infighting, and heavy-handed politics, the strain on employees is often reflected in their weariness.

You find a certain added zest within prisons where the staff members feel a sense of community. It is not just a job with the external compensations of pay and position; being part of the organization holds significant internal rewards. It feels good to belong to and be part of the group. It makes people want to accomplish something, to give something back, to make their own personal contributions. Personnel feel enthusiastic and optimistic about what they can accomplish. In prisons with a healthy sense of community, more tinkering and experimentation occur. Staff pay more attention to improvement, whether in conditions, programs, or ways of doing things.

The trust associated with community brings down the barriers of self-protection that one finds in less benevolent and more predatory settings. Within communities, support more commonly occurs than reprisal. Not having to be on guard about what they say, staff are free to act, make decisions, and solve problems.

Prisons that operate as communities have higher energy levels because people are not afraid to act.

A Common Purpose Which Forms the Basis for a Shared Culture

Thomas Watson, founder of IBM, stated: "I firmly believe that any organization, in order to survive and achieve success, must have a sound set of beliefs on which it premises all its policies and actions."[2] Watson's words seem almost self-evident. Indeed, how can an organization which lacks a fundamental purpose survive? Yet, more often than one might expect, organizations lose their sense of purpose. It happens when an industry's mission shifts from making a product to making money. It happens when employees define their success as moving up the ladder rather than service and contribution to clients and coworkers. It happens when members lower in the organization recognize that they have little influence on what takes place in the organization and start working simply to draw a paycheck. It happens when the goal of the organization becomes survival in a hostile economic or political environment. In the prison business, it happens when the goal becomes "keeping the lid on it," escaping official scrutiny, and avoiding public dissension among staff.

The act of forming an organization necessarily involves the making of value commitments—choosing the nature of the enterprise, its distinctive purpose, approach, and objectives.[3] From an organization's inception, these goals can be displaced. Because a sense of community heightens awareness among staff to their interdependence and gives credence to their identity, it helps maintain attention on the organization's underlying purpose. Communities emerge from a shared history and tradition and unfold in a common set of norms and values. As such, they support and protect the basic philosophy, spirit, and drive of the institution.

In their study of top performing corporations, Peters and Waterman found consistency in dominant values:

1. A belief in being the "best."
2. A belief in the importance of the details of execution, the nuts and bolts of doing the job well.

3. A belief in the importance of people as individuals.
4. A belief in superior quality and service.
5. A belief that most members of the organization should be innovators.
6. A belief in the importance of informality to enhance communication.[4]

Organizations represent their sense of community through symbols and myths. During the year that I spent as a visiting fellow at the Federal Bureau of Prisons, I often heard members of that organization refer to the Bureau as the best-run prison system in the world. The Director made reference to this distinction in a ceremony to recognize outstanding service among employees, but I also overheard Bureau employees allude to the organization's superiority when they talked about how they did their jobs. Whether accurate or not, belief in being number one is a powerful motivator. It serves as a constant guide for performance and sets a high standard by which to judge oneself.

Uplifting and Fulfilling Climate

In their research on correctional officers, Poole and Regoli found considerable evidence of social isolation among officers. They observed both a lack of an extensive work camaraderie and in-group solidarity. One might not expect this finding. Like police officers, correctional officers experience fear in working with potentially violent individuals and perceive themselves to lack the support of superiors and the public. Consequently, one might expect correctional officers to develop a closely knit subculture, characterized by cohesion and self-protection, as police officers have. Poole and Regoli found little evidence of such affiliation.[5]

Two aspects of prison work apparently resist the development of strong alliances among staff. First, correctional officers often work alone. Interactions with fellow officers are restricted to brief work-related encounters. Second, many prison systems endorse a work ethic of high personal accountability. Administrators and fellow workers expect correctional officers to be self-reliant and to perform their duties autonomously. As Fleisher suggests in his book about the U.S. prison at Lompoc, California: "A penitentiary culture systematically isolates insiders from insiders. The time-honored inmate expression, 'do your own time,' also applies to staff."[6] Evidence to the contrary is viewed as a sign of weakness and as an indication that an individual cannot manage inmates. Together, these two features of prison work act to limit teamwork and prevent collective and cooperative approaches to problem solving.   Correctional officers work independently, without allegiance to the overall mission of the prison organization.[7]

Such fragmentation among workers flies directly in the face of what we know about effective organizations. Effective prisons fashion a sense of identity and belonging and foster mutual trust and loyalty among employees.

An important aspect of a fulfilling work environment is having fun, yet the very idea of "having fun" seems antithetical to the business of running prisons. If you are having fun, can you really be taking your job seriously? But having fun is not limited to playing around. In a study of corporate employees, accomplishing goals, getting positive results, and being in a group were found to be related to perceptions of "having fun." The study discovered that employees who reported having fun were less anxious and depressed, more satisfied with their jobs, more motivated, more creative, and better able to meet the demands of their jobs.[8]

Research dating back to the Hawthorne studies has demonstrated the power of group dynamics, both positive and negative. Depending on the cohesiveness of the group and the relationship of informal norms to the goals of the organization, productivity may be increased or decreased accordingly. Highly cohesive groups tend to exceed average levels of performance when they accept the goals of the organization, but fall below average levels of performance when they reject organizational goals. Research has shown that individuals who are comfortable with their coworkers and find fulfillment in interacting with them are less likely to be absent or to terminate their employment.[9]

Contribution and Service

Members of organizations enter into a covenant (sometimes consciously, but often not) to meet their collective needs by fulfilling the needs of one another. If you think about it, the fundamental reason for forming groups is so individuals can more effectively and efficiently realize their own needs; otherwise, little reason for organizing exists. Members pool their talents, energies, and resources to produce something that would be impossible for a single individual to produce as efficiently.

By their very nature, contribution and service characterize relationships within organizational communities. Members recognize that they need one another and see themselves as having a positive duty to contribute to the organization and to serve others. This requires that individuals move beyond their narrow self-interests to consider the needs of the group. At times, individuals must sacrifice their own requirements, placing the good of the group ahead of their own wants and desires.

As we saw in the previous chapter, individuals work for the good of the whole when they feel they have some stake in it. That comes from seeing the larger picture and assuming ownership for some portion of the enterprise.

Obviously, harmony and the spirit of cooperation and mutual support do not always typify prison organizations. Rivalry, competition, and undermining actions develop among organizational members and functional units because they have different and competing interests.

Within a prison, correctional officers view security and order as primary goals that cannot be compromised. Alternatively, treatment staff may view individual freedom of expression as therapeutically beneficial to inmates. Ideally (in well-functioning prison communities), custody and treatment support one another. Custody produces a safe environment in which treatment can occur; treatment provides inmates with something to do which decreases the likelihood that they will get into trouble. If staff fail to resolve the conflict between security and freedom of expression, then the mutual support of custody and treatment will be undermined. Correctional officers sabotage the efforts of treatment staff by playing "mind games" until inmates react violently and must be restrained. Treatment staff openly express their disrespect for correctional officers which supports inmates' resistance to custodial authority.

For contribution and service to remain viable aspects of the prison community, compromise and coalition building are essential. Leaders must pay constant attention to renewing a sense of community.

Problem Solving, Conflict Resolution, and Governance

Well-functioning organizational communities have momentum, which derives from the mutual belief among a group of people that their welfare is interrelated and that they should work together toward an agreed-upon goal. Momentum develops when organizational members endorse an image of what they want to be, develop a strategy to get there, and conceive of a way of directing and controlling their progress toward that objective. That requires governance, yet political behavior within an organization is a difficult beast to control.

Where upward mobility dominates, approval-seeking behavior replaces the group's momentum and competition rather than cooperation becomes the norm. The success of others threatens our own ambitions. Helping others harms our chances of success. So we become strategic in our actions, manipulating situations to our own personal advantage, telling bosses what they want to hear, reluctantly sharing information with peers, and trusting no one. In this way, a traditional bureaucracy feeds upon itself. Premised on a lack of trust, the system promotes a lack of trust, which in turn strengthens the belief that people cannot be trusted and must be controlled.

Organizations that work as communities find alternative ways of governing themselves that stress cooperation rather than competition, trust, commitment, and a willingness to put the welfare of the organization first. Collaboration is sought in which all employees share power, risk, and accountability.

Leaders Make a Difference

During a prison crisis, a sense of community often occurs in an instant, but over the long haul, community does not simply happen. It must be nurtured and renewed. Prison leaders can begin to make a difference in the way prisons operate by working to build a sense of community, encouraging teamwork and collaborative problem solving, and urging cooperation. The most successful leaders serve as catalysts by lifting people out of their individual self-interests and uniting them toward more lofty goals.[11]

To build community, leaders begin with a common, unifying theme or principle among people. Luckily, as we have noted, the elements of motivation already reside within people—we all want to accomplish something worthwhile, to do new things, to learn and develop new skills, to be tested, and to do something of which we can be proud. Leaders read their people and ignite within them that spark that results in higher levels of performance. To do this requires leaders to be good *followers*.

The idea of leaders as followers contradicts a common notion of leaders as strong individualists who singlehandedly solve problems. In fact, it has been my observation that effective leaders model good team behavior; they carefully listen to what people say, what they need, and what they value. This requires an exceedingly "hands-on" style, where leaders spend considerable time walking through their facilities, talking to staff and listening to their replies. Leaders capitalize on that information and begin to weave the social fabric of community among their people. They give meaning to the enterprise of incarcerating people, how it is going to be done, and what is going to be accomplished.[12]

Meaning is often created at the point where language and culture intersect. It is not a trivial outcome that the Federal Bureau of Prisons refers to itself as a family. Metaphors play significant roles in determining what is real and how reality gets defined.[13] By referring to itself as a family, the Bureau implies a special kind of closeness and concern, a way of relating to one another, and a lifelong connectedness. "Family" serves as a powerful image for members of the Bureau about how they will be treated within what could otherwise be a large and impersonal bureaucracy.

Leaders use metaphors, and language in general, to give meaning to what goes on in the organization. You should select your language carefully. Seldom indulge in the luxury of speaking for yourself alone.[14] Instead, focus on the higher order values that bind people together. In articulating a common ground, avoid being too specific to be as encompassing as possible. Leave room for diversity in beliefs among people and allow them to be creative in how the job will be done. Be positive. Be optimistic. But also be genuine and honest. Recognize the hardships and difficulties that staff face, but inspire people to prevail and triumph.[15] People want capable and strong leaders upon whom they can depend. This requires leaders to be clear in their own minds about their beliefs. It is essential that leaders not vacillate, but that they be willing to compromise.

Leaders make a difference in how community gets defined by modeling reciprocity. I know a teacher who strongly advocates participatory management as a leadership style for criminal justice organizations, but let one of his students question his authority in the classroom and he is outraged. The inconsistency of his rhetoric and action does not long escape his students. Leaders have an obligation to set an example of how they want others to act. If you want them to trust you, trust them. If you want them to be committed, be committed to them.

With a position of leadership comes power. The desire for power, in itself, is *not* a bad thing. The need provides the motivation for taking responsibility, directing others, and achieving group objectives. Power can be expressed in a desire to see an organization succeed or the people within it grow. Here, we are talking about power in service of others. Alternatively, some individuals seek power to assuage their egos. Followers generally see through leader's solitary pursuits of prestige and grandeur. They may follow the leader's orders, but will lack true commitment to the leader's purpose.

Kouzes and Posner distinguish leaders who have a "personalized" power concern from those who have a "socialized" power concern. The latter exercise power to benefit others. They tend to be less egotistical and more emotionally mature, less likely to be manipulative and controlling, less defensive, and willing to sacrifice self-interests for the good of the group.[16] Max Depree suggests that "the first responsibility of a leader is to define reality. The last is to say thank you. In between the two, the leader must become a servant and a debtor." Leaders should be stewards of the organization and its people, being personally responsible for its momentum, effectiveness, civility and values, and for leaving a legacy.[17]

One can begin to model reciprocity by making liberal use of the word "we" in conversation. When referring to future institutional directions, talk about *our* plans; when you have accomplished something, share the credit. You cannot do the job alone. To be successful, enlist people as *partners* in whatever task, project, or activity you undertake. Be warned, however. People see through hypocrisy. If you are going to use the word *we*, then plans clearly must be mutually defined and developed, not dictated by you alone.

The second thing one can do to model reciprocity is get to know people. Don't remain distant and aloof. Talk to them. Be engaging. And, be interested in them as unique people. Be a friend when you can. Support them and show your concern. That's what it means to be "family."

When interacting with people on a personal level, leaders should acknowledge their contributions to the group dynamic. Recognize and reward loyalty. Encourage individuals who have the kind of personality that contributes to team spirit.

In larger prison systems, staff tend to move from facility to facility as they advance within the organization. As a result, few mid- and upper-level managers have resided at their present institution for very long. In contrast to these highly mobile professional managers, some prison staff end up staying at the same facility. In some cases, these individuals remain stationary after reaching a plateau in their careers, but others choose to remain where they are for personal or family reasons.

In some prisons, the mobile professionals impute, often subtly, a secondary status to stationary staff, believing them to be less capable or less dedicated to the organization because of their unwillingness to make the self-sacrifice of moving. Making such a distinction divides the community and ignores the important contribution that stationary staff make. Some stationary staff serve as the "elders" of the institution; they understand its culture and are influential within the informal networks of the staff. They recognize the personality quirks of different staff and capably maneuver through the mire of local bureaucracy. Stationary staff are the purveyors of institutional history, the storytellers, and the influentials among the local crowd. They often have the most influence on new staff. Make stationary staff part of the team, recognize their talents, and reward their contributions and you strengthen the community; disrespect them, and the community will be divided.

Building Teams

Leaders must foster collaboration by creating and sustaining cooperative goals. This requires leaders to pay as much attention to how group members relate to one another as they attend to the tasks at hand. There are five rather straightforward activities by which you can encourage collaboration and teamwork:

Create Interactions

Line staff and supervisors expect self-reliance among correctional officers. This custom does not bode well for developing a healthy organizational community and effective teams. Prison executives need to find ways of making certain that staff do not work in isolation, that they interact, learn to depend upon one another, and support one another.

Because many prison employees work a solitary station, in a tower, at a particular gate, and even in a classroom or a counselor's office, administrators need to provide opportunities for them to associate and socialize. The sense of community will be heightened as people get to know one another and begin to interact across disciplinary boundaries. The promotion of such interactions is one of the most positive benefits of unit management. Interdisciplinary teams interact regularly and are charged with arranging inmates' activities and programs across the institution.

For example, when J. Michael Quinlan was warden of the Federal Correctional Institution at Otisville, he used group projects to build morale. The projects brought people together, challenged them, and in the end gave them a sense of accomplishment. Group involvement in problem solving generally produces a better solution, but, importantly, also fosters collaboration. People get to know one another. They learn about the difficulties others face in doing their particular jobs. Interaction begets further interaction, serving as the basis for future collaborative activities and problem solving.

Share Information

Prison executives have traditionally provided information to their staff on a "need-to-know" basis. But as Tom Peters suggests in his book, *Thriving on Chaos*, sharing information is a powerfully liberating force within an organization.[18] Leaders need to let people know about their plans and ideas, and about what's going on in the facility and with management. Only then can staff react, contribute, provide valuable feedback and support, and prepare for change.

When leaders shield people below them in the organization from bad news, they are acting in a paternalistic manner, not trusting their people to handle the information properly. When leaders shield people above them, they act like a child, fearing reprisal for bearing bad news. Leaders must make the people below and above them partners in the enterprise.[19] Several benefits result from sharing information:

1. It confirms that the institution considers all employees to be partners and problem solvers.

2. Having information readily available forms the basis for day-to-day problem solving. Without knowledge of the problem, it is unlikely that someone will take responsibility for it.

3. Sharing information prevents upper-level power plays because issues are better understood by all parties.

4. Posting information encourages and speeds action taking.

5. Information begets information.

6. Information sharing helps flatten the organizational structure by increasing interaction across functional boundaries.[20]

Delegate

Most people who end up prison executives are self-starters, have considerable energy and intelligence, and believe themselves to be competent. They work their way up the organization and are used to taking considerable responsibility for getting the job done. That's good, because running prisons is difficult and challenging. But such competence becomes problematic when executives fail to delegate and try to singlehandedly run their facilities or units. A few executives are so competent and so energetic that they can successfully do this for awhile; however, they are not helping their organizations because they are failing to develop the next generation of leaders.

Rather than not delegating, more administrators run into the problem of *conditionally delegating*. They give staff members responsibility for a task but fail to extend full authority and freedom to carry out those responsibilities. Arising from the need to retain control and assure predictability, these managers never really let go. Instead, they require staff members to report back before making major decisions or keep checking up on the project and making suggestions. Staff get caught between really running with the project and accommodating the boss. A tension arises that neither supports leadership development nor self-fulfillment.

Conditional delegation conveys the message that "I really don't trust you. I'm giving you a task to do, but I lack sufficient confidence in you to leave you alone." That message denies ownership and encourages passivity and dependence. Only with *true* delegation will staff become empowered and deeply committed to the project. Noted psychologist Carl Rogers observed that trusting someone's competence, judgment, helpfulness, and concern results in greater openness.[21] True delegation promotes a climate of reciprocity that supports teamwork.

Note that over-delegation can be as problematic as under-delegation. Leaders who over-delegate run the risk of abdicating their responsibilities; they lose sight of overall operations and cannot contribute to the project. They give their staff the impression of not caring, of not being involved. In the end, no one may be in charge.

Create a Climate of Trust

Trust may be the most important ingredient of teamwork. Without it, the team can never really come together; communication is difficult, information gets distorted, misinterpreted, and is misunderstood. Members engage in self-protection and are suspicious and unreceptive to one another. Genuine openness cannot develop because team members do not know whether they can rely upon one another. Researchers have found trust to be the single most important element in an individual's job satisfaction.[22]

Trust begins with the leader. To be trusted, one must be trustworthy. One must meet commitments and keep promises to be regarded as dependable.

Trust evolves from five essential ingredients: respect, truthfulness, reliability, fairness, and genuineness. To *respect* someone, a leader must appreciate and value the individual's contribution to the organization. One of the quickest ways to sever a relationship is to publicly ridicule a person. Ridicule shames the individual in a way that makes it difficult for that individual to ever feel secure again.

Other less drastic reactions than ridicule may also be interpreted to indicate a lack of respect. Yelling at staff members, constantly shooting down their ideas, not listening, putting them off, and talking behind their backs all suggest that one has little consideration for their feelings. The likely reaction of personnel who feel that a leader doesn't respect them is not to respect the leader in return.

People vary in their intelligence, competence, and reliability. It would be wonderful if we had to work with only the most intelligent, most competent, and most reliable individuals; yet, as we all know, this is never the case. As a leader, one must find ways to appreciate the contributions of *all* employees and to help even the least proficient persons grow to their full potential.

The second essential ingredient for building trust is *truthfulness*. Trust is a fragile entity. If a leader betrays it with a lie, trust is almost impossible to regain. From that point on, others will never know for sure whether the individual is being truthful or not. A nagging suspicion will linger that the leader will be dishonest again.

Reliability serves as the third element in building trust. Being consistent gives people a notion of what to expect. It creates predictability in their world. People need to know that leaders will do what they say—that what's important today will be important tomorrow. When a leader acts as a loose cannon crashing about the ship, people become cautious, defensive, and strategic.

Trust also grows where *fairness* predominates. Having a decision go against you is never pleasant, but having it go against you unfairly is alienating. A leader's decisions should be equitable, impartial, unbiased, and unprejudiced. To avoid being taken as unfair, one should be open and forthcoming with the reasons for decisions. Let people know the criteria used.

Genuineness is the final element in building trust. I worked for an administrator at my university who often stated that his primary responsibility is to serve faculty and students. But this individual's actions belied his rhetoric. He reveled in power plays and seemed to enjoy making decisions that went against someone. This administrator was one of the least trusted individuals on campus.

Deception is usually seen for what it really is: manipulation, a way of getting people to do what we want them to do without their knowing it. My administrator wanted people to trust him. His soothing words of service were initially ingratiating, but the first time you got caught up in one of his power plays you never trusted him again. Not being genuine means being indirect, devious, and closed in one's relations with others.

Being genuine also involves admitting our mistakes and exposing our weaknesses. Some executives feel that by revealing their vulnerabilities they may be seen as weak and ineffective. More likely, they will be regarded as human, approachable, and trustworthy.[23] Trust builds reciprocity. It signals people that they can allow themselves to be open and vulnerable, that they are not going to be taken advantage of or blind-sided.

Celebrate Accomplishment

As ambitious, hard working, and self-confident leaders, our inclination is to push onward, planning, developing, and constantly striving for improvement. When I completed my Ph.D. dissertation, I was shocked by how anticlimactic it felt. After working so long and so hard, I expected to feel a sense of relief and accomplishment. Instead, I felt as though I had lost a part of my life and did not quite know what to do with myself. It is important to pause and recognize one's accomplishments, to revel in them, and to celebrate.

Celebrations help build teams. They create positive interactions that recognize and honor the ability of the group to work together and to achieve something of significance. Celebrations build solidarity and reaffirm beliefs. Leaders can use celebrations as opportunities to acknowledge actions they consider important.

Each year, institutions develop elaborate lists of objectives to be accomplished, many of which the staff successfully achieves, only to rebuild their list once again as they enter yet another new year. Unless they stop to pat themselves on the back, that process will soon become mundane and not all that gratifying. Celebration builds vitality and enthusiasm. It makes hard work seem worthwhile and fun. It helps people feel good about themselves and close to their fellow workers.

Leaders should plan regular and formal recognition events where they celebrate the service and accomplishments of the staff and the organization. They should reward Herculean efforts and acknowledge the sorts of behavior they want to encourage. But some celebrations should be more informal, giving people the opportunity to have fun, to interact, and to praise and congratulate one another.

The one essential component of recognition is sincerity. Phil Spears, former federal prison warden and now Deputy Regional Director, Northeast Region, still remembers when he received his 5-year pin—in the mail and with his name misspelled! To say the least, he didn't feel that anyone had acknowledged his accomplishment, nor did he feel all that good about his organization.

Perhaps, the most powerful form of recognition is a simple, "thank you." It means that someone has recognized your efforts and appreciates them. It conveys the message that you are not working alone, that you are contributing to the team, and that your contribution is valued. It serves as a public acclaim of important values: to do something well, to accomplish something, to be tested, to contribute, and to be part of the group.

Alignment

This and the previous chapter have been about how leaders can motivate, inspire, and energize people to perform extraordinarily in their jobs and to achieve ambitious goals. We have talked about how to get people to take ownership and to work effectively as teams. But, be warned, the tactic can misfire.

A few years ago, assertiveness training became popular in many organizations. Because many clerical workers felt powerless and alienated, they were particularly targeted for such training. Assertiveness training is aimed at increasing individuals' sense of personal power and encourages them not to be passive, to be self-expressive, and to assert their rights. This is all well and good, except assertiveness training did little to modify clerical workers' position within the organization. It did not make them more powerful nor did it alleviate the alienating aspect of their jobs. As a result, assertiveness training often simply empowered angry, alienated clerical employees to state their frustrations.

To achieve the kind of extraordinary performance we have been referring to, teams must be aligned—that is, all headed in the same direction—as well as empowered. But, simply agreeing on where we want the organization to go is not enough; that happens every time people get together and plan. Extraordinary performance comes when people feel a deep personal commitment to a vision of the organization and dedicate themselves to achieving it. Team members unite around a common vision.[24]

Diversity

America's workforce is changing. By the end of the century, 85 percent of all new workers will be women and minorities. This trend has significant implications for the management of prisons whose workers historically have been predominantly white males.

Traditionally, both corporate America and law enforcement have promoted *sameness*, or uniformity, among workers. Conformity, exactness, and predictability helped assure a high degree of control and efficiency. With the changing workforce, however, such a model is no longer possible or appropriate. Scotsmen, Dutchmen, and Frenchmen could reach a level of sameness that is simply not possible for blacks, Asians, and women, and that is an organizational value to which new workers are not willing to conform.

For example, when prisons were predominantly male organizations, the issue of child care could be ignored. Now that women have joined the ranks and, in many cases, both fathers and mothers are employed in the same institution, the provision of child care is an issue prisons must consider.

Respect for cultural diversity within the workforce offers two advantages over the promotion of uniformity. First, it holds the promise of producing better ideas. When women first sought the right to be law enforcement and correctional officers in male facilities, there was considerable resistance to their employment. The chief argument against their inclusion: women are not strong enough to restrain larger, physically stronger, agitated males. Thus, their inclusion in the workforce would pose a significant risk for both the female officer and her male counterparts who would have to come to her defense. Women eventually won the right in the courts to be law enforcement and correctional officers, and as it turned out, research indicates that they are more successful than men in handling agitated offenders and inmates. Rather than intensifying aggressive situations, female officers more likely calm the situation and thus avoid the need for physical restraint. Thus, inclusion of women in the force led to a better method for handling agitated individuals.

The second advantage of respect for cultural differences is reduced alienation with consequent enhanced productivity. Even with an all white male workforce, considerable human costs were associated with promotion of uniformity. It often meant not respecting the employee's individuality and uniqueness.

As a contemporary manager, if you hope to create a sense of community among your people, you are going to have to respect and recognize their diversity. But, how do you do that? Here are some suggestions.

First off, recognize that there is no single right way to do things, particularly if that way is always your way! Create a safe, trusting, and respectful climate in which people feel free to express their opinions. To do that, you must be able to deal effectively with opinions that oppose or conflict with your own.

Next, work on being a good communicator. Be clear and direct and give honest feedback. Try to understand and accept others' frames of reference, and recognize that there can be more than one view of the world based upon a person's own experiences and background. Also promote open and respectful communication within your organization or unit.

Third, strive to extend your understanding and appreciation of cultural diversity. Learn about the history and reality of groups with different cultural backgrounds than your own. For example, you may be trying to improve morale and productivity within your unit by publicly praising your people when they do a good job. However, if you have an Asian or American Indian employee, you may find that his or her performance will decline if you praise the individual. Within some cultural groups, public praise is embarrassing and to be avoided.

Next, endeavor to remove barriers that may limit inclusion. That means that you will have to effectively manage conflict, complexity, and change within your organization. Not only must you change but you must help others to change as well.

The reality is that diversity is upon us; the reward for dealing with it is organizations with greater trust and respect, less alienation, and more adaptability.

6

PULLING IT TOGETHER

Ostensibly, from the time they were created until the late 1960s, prisons were ruled by the authoritarian control of the custody force. Within these paramilitary regimes, power was attached to position within the chain of command. The warden served as the ultimate ruler who often exercised totalitarian command of the institution, its staff, and the prisoners. Control was maintained by a rigid set of rules and unflagging discipline for staff and prisoners alike. Guards regulated the behavior of prisoners through the discretionary enforcement of rules and the virtually unchecked use of punishment and force.

Life within these traditional institutions was relatively simple. Guards had one primary responsibility: to maintain security and ensure internal order. Rules and regulations detailed expectations for appropriate behavior of prisoners. A complementary set of policy directed guards in their surveillance of prisoners and the enforcement of rules.[1] The paramount goal of *order* was clearly articulated and explicitly pursued.

During the 1960s and early 70s, several changes occurred which drastically, and irretrievably, altered life within the traditional prison.[2] Interest in rehabilitation led to employment of a new set of prison workers: educated professionals whose goals included the treatment and transformation of inmates. Their appearance within the institution challenged the traditional authority of the custody force to autocratically control the inmate population. These new professionals argued that positive change of inmates could not be successfully achieved within the highly coercive atmosphere of the traditional institution. Instead, a more therapeutic setting was needed in which inmates would be free to express themselves and to pursue their own personal development.

Under rehabilitation, the role of institutional custody was modified. Custodial staff were no longer called "guards" but were retitled "correctional officers." Responsibilities were expanded to include supporting the individual reform of each inmate. Exactly how to integrate the new role of treatment with the traditional one of maintaining order proved to be unclear, contradictory, and impossible for many officers. In the hope of creating relaxed and friendly relations, many prisons eliminated specific rules of conduct. While inmates were not allowed to act in any manner they pleased, and escape and threats to staff and other inmate safety were not tolerated, the handling of behavior outside these broadly defined areas was left to the officers' discretion. Many correctional officers felt a sense of futility and frustration being thrust into such an ambiguous role.[3]

In concurrent and related action to the emphasis of rehabilitation within prisons, the courts began to address constitutional issues of prisoners' rights in the 1960s. Judicial decisions redressed the use of physical coercion and force by correctional officers, arbitrary decision-making, and the absence of procedural guidelines and rights of due process. Each of these actions chipped away at the traditional system of control and the unmitigated power of the guard force.

In response to changing social conditions outside the walls, inmates and correctional officers became more politicized. Initially, inmates organized, resisted, and openly defied custodial authority, and they occasionally rioted. Much of the protest centered around control and power. Often times, what may have begun as associations of inmates with legitimate grievances deteriorated into the predatory and violent gangs that endure in many contemporary institutions.[4]

In several prison systems, correctional officers responded to the changing political environment by seeking greater power through unionization. When successful, this action severed the traditional, strict hierarchical organization of the custodial force by segregating management and line functions.

Each of these actions—the introduction of rehabilitation, court intervention, politicization of the inmates, and the unionization of the correctional officers—started out with the goal of creating safer and more humane prisons. However, the overall effect has often been the opposite and, consequently, has been labeled the "paradox of reform."[5] The degeneration of the inmate social order and an escalation of violence have often followed on the heels of reform. One writer claims that staff demoralization and disorganization led to a demise in security and that the rehabilitation ideal resulted in worse living conditions and few programmatic opportunities.[6]

Controversy has arisen among prison researchers about the safety of contemporary institutions in contrast to traditional prisons. Some observers claim that a more dangerous environment resulted from reforms, whereas others claim that while an initial spike in the level of violence may have followed reform, overall prisons are no less safe today than in the past.[7] Clearly, some facilities came out of the chaotic times of 1960s and 70s better than others.

I visited a facility in which the buildings that once housed active and productive industries had been converted to dormitories. A well-meaning, past warden believed that work in industries detracted from the establishment of a therapeutic community and closed all programs. The therapeutic environment, however, was never realized and few treatment programs remain. Overcrowding forced the facility to convert the buildings into housing units. Now, idleness prevails among the inmates; they roam the compound with little to do, other than engage in prohibited activities. Out of fear, correctional officers hang back in sallyports and other protected areas. Administrators seldom walk through the facility.

In contrast, I have visited prisons in which the social order remains very much intact. Inmates work in industry or are assigned to programs and other jobs. Staff contain violence and the distribution of contraband within acceptable limits. The facilities are clean and programs are well-run. From my perspective, the key to whether the social order continued to deteriorate or was restored is effective leadership.

James Jacobs in his study of the Illinois prison, Statesville, reached a similar conclusion:

> The crisis in control that enveloped Statesville between 1970 and 1975 threatened to overwhelm the prison because the advocates of the rehabilitative ideology were unable to build an administration which defined duties and obligations, focused responsibility, and rationalized its procedures.[8]

The administrator who turned Statesville around endorsed scientific principles of management that enabled him to develop good relations with the various contingencies within the prison. He attempted to run a safe, clean, and program-oriented facility that did not violate the law, administrative regulations, or court mandates. The warden strengthened security, enhanced services, and revitalized staff morale. He downplayed the use of punishment for violators, concentrating instead on restraining individuals who posed a threat to institutional security.[9]

Building Success

In October 1990, the RAND Corporation published the results of its study of successful urban high schools. The report, entitled "High Schools With Character: Alternatives to Bureaucracy," studied 13 New York City schools serving largely minority and economically disadvantaged students. Included were Catholic, specialized public, and neighborhood schools.[10]

Successful high schools (ones in which 80 percent of the students graduated, and a high percentage took college entrance exams and scored relatively well) placed heavy emphasis on student achievement, were determined to mold attitudes and values, operated as relatively independent problem-solving organizations, and had a primary commitment to students, parents, and the neighborhood. In contrast, regular high schools (where 50 percent of the students graduated and a small percent took college entrance exams and did well) had diffuse programs, let students and faculty define their own roles, were internally rigid, and emphasized compliance with bureaucratic regulations and accountability to higher authorities. In other words, successful schools emphasize quality and commitment to their mission. They accept a high degree of responsibility to serve their constituents—students, parents, and the neighborhood. They possess a few fundamental values, including student achievement and moral development. Having this orientation, successful schools operate as problem solvers, working through issues to achieve their well-articulated mission.

Regular schools operate as functional bureaucracies, maintaining rigid internal divisions of labor and emphasizing compliance with regulations defined by central bureaucracies. Teachers agree not to demand too much of students in return for the students' agreement not to cause too much trouble.[11]

I will not belabor the point by making the obvious connection between successful schools and successful prisons but will note the historical context of prison organizations. Prisons traditionally were organized and administered as authoritarian custodial regimes. In the 1960s, a variety of social forces—internal and external to the prison organization—intruded on the autocratic dominion of custody, resulting in the fragmentation of its power. Prisons sought to reorganize themselves into reform-oriented, therapeutic communities or, in some cases, into democratically governed polities where staff and inmates shared responsibility for governance. From my perspective, both attempts failed.[12]

Some prisons evolved from this "crisis in control" into functional bureaucracies much like the regular schools described above. Rather than making their primary commitment to their constituents—inmates, staff, and the local community—and functioning in a problem-solving mode to provide high quality incarceration, they function as rigid bureaucracies which strive to comply with rules and regulations imposed by a central office. This philosophy trickles down within the institution so that compliance with regulations serves as a model for staff behavior throughout the facility. Typically, such prisons maintain rigid divisions of labor between functional areas with little crossover and communication.

Other prisons spun out of the crisis of control and selected a mode of operation similar to that of the successful schools. They are committed to a few well-defined values and goals (e.g., security, services, and good staff morale) which are oriented toward meeting the needs of their constituents rather than bureaucratically defined regulations. Inmates and staff are held accountable to these standards. Practice is problem-oriented, constantly seeking ways of realizing goals. Taking responsibility and initiative are expected. There is general acceptance by the staff of the principle that they owe the public, inmates, and themselves high quality incarceration, which they have a duty to provide. Staff harken to this commitment rather than to externally defined regulations.

Making It Happen

The preceding discussion takes us full circle back to the suggestion made in the introduction to this section that successful prisons emphasize tight but loose properties. Well-run prisons, on one hand, are rigidly controlled and characterized by firm central direction. Simultaneously and paradoxically, well-run facilities also allow staff autonomy to do their jobs well. The moral prescription to the delivery of high quality incarceration allows a problem-oriented, rather than bureaucratically regulated, practice to develop. Prison executives can take four key steps toward improving their operations: (1) establish a few key principles, (2) mute functional boundaries, (3) emphasize responsibility, commitment, and teamwork, and (4) encourage an entrepreneurial spirit.

Establish a Few Key Principles

If you want a well-run facility, you must know what one looks like. When I work with prisons to help facilitate their development of yearly strategic plans, I begin with the question, "What constitutes high quality incarceration?" I ask people to describe the characteristics of a well-run prison. We then develop plans to maintain those characteristics that the staff feel their facility possesses. Where the facility falls short of the criterion, we discuss what needs to be done to move to a higher level of care and custody. In these discussions, I find considerable consensus about what constitutes quality incarceration. I detected few systematic differences in the opinions of employees at different levels within institutions or among staff located at different prisons. Everyone working in prisons generally agrees that well-run facilities are clean and sanitary, that they are safe and orderly, that the food and health care are good, that inmates are not idle but are productively involved in programming, institutional maintenance, and industry, and that staff morale is high.

Yet, there is considerable variation that exists among prisons in how closely they come to achieving such a widely agreed upon standard. From less successful institutions, I hear several excuses: (1) lack of resources, (2) interference and restrictions imposed by central office policy, and (3) the union. At well-run prisons, I hear staff throughout the facilities articulate these standards, whereas at the less well-run places, no one mentions them.

A prison CEO, department head, or unit manager can begin paying attention to these standards in a couple of ways. Since near universal consensus about them exists, the executive could walk into the next staff meeting with a list and tell people that these things are important. Alternatively, the executive could walk into the next staff meeting with a pad of newsprint and initiate a discussion about what a well-run facility looks like. Then, he or she could compare present conditions with the ideal and begin brainstorming about how to get from where they are to where they would like to be. The second approach has the advantage of building ownership, of giving people a say in what's recognized as important.

I used to walk into my college classes the first day of each semester and hand out a syllabus which briefly described the course objectives, laid out a schedule for the semester, and specified the requirements. I stopped doing this a few years ago. Now, the students and I develop the syllabus together. After several semesters, I consistently find that the syllabi developed with students have the same general objectives and course content that I would have stipulated had I developed the courses independently. The only difference, and this may surprise some readers, is that the students usually impose more stringent course requirements than I would have. At the end of the semester in an anonymous review, I ask students what effect my asking them to share responsibility for the design and implementation of the class had on them. No students have ever stated that they disliked the method. Their feedback generally runs along the lines of: "it increased my desire to learn," "it motivated me to keep up with the work," "it breaks down the barriers," "it was satisfying and educationally beneficial," "you showed respect for us."

I recognize that most prisons develop yearly plans. I've read them: (1) increase housing capacity by 75 beds, (2) renovate A and G unit showers, (3) replace concertina wire with razor wire around the perimeter, and so forth. Yearly strategic plans tend to document what is already happening and deal with physical development and renovation of the facility. They fail to inspire a new vision to which the institution should strive; that comes from recognizing the importance of sticking to the basics, jointly identifying those few simple but fundamental principles associated with quality incarceration, making them part of institutional culture, and doggedly pursuing them.

Deemphasize Functional Boundaries

If you had a conversation with a staff member at a typical institution and asked about who is responsible for various functions within the facility, the conversation might go something like this. What's the most important thing in running a prison? Institutional security, of course. Whose responsibility is security? Well, that's custody's responsibility. What else is important? Having some programs for inmates is important. That keeps them busy and gives them a chance for self-improvement. Who's responsible for programs? The Deputy for Programs is in charge, and he works with the education, recreation, and counseling departments to provide these services. What else is important? Staff need to get paid regularly, and the prison needs to accurately keep up with time-served by the inmates. Those are the responsibilities of the folks in administration. And so the story goes since prisons have first been built. Institutions have clearly defined divisions of functional responsibility.

I do not deny the importance of having a division of labor within prison organizations. The tasks to be performed in contemporary institutions are diverse and require considerable skill and expertise. Indeed, someone must be assigned responsibility for the tasks if we want to assure their timely completion.

But organizations, much like humans, pass through developmental stages as they mature. Organizations tend to become rigid over time, adding administrative complexity, layers of middle managers, and rules and regulations to control, standardize, and order operations. This bureaucratization of the institution leads to reductions in adaptability, innovation, and good communication, which, in turn, leaves many prison workers feeling stifled, alienated, sometimes angry, and without a sense of how their behavior fits into the whole. Staff do their own time. Even when there is not an active labor/management dispute, staff "work to rule," performing their jobs as explicitly set out by policy. Little interaction across functional boundaries occurs. Compliance with regulations becomes more important than solving problems.

What can leaders do to sway this tide? Eliminating the division of labor, policies, and regulations will not solve the problem, but would simply replace the drift toward rigidity with disorder and chaos. But, when prison managers stress the rules and regulations too much, the procedures and routines become more important than the original purpose of providing high quality incarceration. My advice is to hold the focus on keeping the place clean and safe rather than on rules and their enforcement. Bend the rules if it will make the facility cleaner or safer! And for goodness sake, make cleanliness and safety everyone's responsibility. In other words, mute who's responsible for the important things so that everyone can feel more personally responsible.

Unit management does this through interdisciplinary teams responsible for *all* aspects of inmates' lives within the facility. Unit management builds expertise and communication across functional boundaries. The system is problem-oriented and gives unit staff decision-making responsibilities. Program flexibility results because treatment plans can be individualized.

Other steps to spread responsibility throughout the facility can be taken. Make security everyone's duty. When an incident occurs, all staff respond—even if it is simply to hold the door open for the special response team. In most prison systems, all staff receive training in security, but some places fail to follow up with constant encouragement for non-custody staff to play an active role in maintaining security, to be vigilant in attention to security breaches, and to communicate those observations.

Keeping inmates involved in programs should also be everyone's responsibility. That means that correctional officers should encourage participation and should praise inmates who receive an A in a class or successfully complete a vocational program. For this to happen, the educational department has to let officers know what is going on.

Cross-disciplinary problem solving is also important. If the completion rate of an educational program drops, involve line correctional officers in figuring out why this is happening and what can be done. That way correctional officers get to know what is going on in education and vice versa. This approach draws on the officers' expertise, challenges them, involves them in decision-making, and gives them something new to do.

One of the greatest shortcomings in prison administration is the lack of a well-designed system of personnel rotation. The federal system is one of the few that regularly moves employees across functional boundaries. One warden and several assistants in the system started out as secretaries. When a bright and ambitious correctional officer completes his college degree, he may be made a personnel specialist. A good teacher may be promoted to a unit manager position.

Several benefits result from this practice. It builds cross-disciplinary expertise. That's important when people end up at the top of the organization. They have more than a single area of expertise and are generally more versatile. It is also important lower down in the organization because it increases understanding and appreciation across functional boundaries. "Cross-breeding" prevents functional areas from becoming too singleminded and can lessen hostilities that might otherwise develop. It also increases communication.

For individuals, personnel rotation provides new and challenging areas of responsibility. It opens up a greater number of possibilities for promotion. People develop new skills and gain a broader perspective of the institution. Personnel rotation prevents stagnation and encourages employees to continue their education.[13]

Emphasize Responsibility, Commitment, and Teamwork

In the previous chapter, I discussed the importance of emphasizing these three traits. To do this, you have to have a genuine interest in people. You must care about their happiness, their well-being, and their advancement within the organization.

In some cases, your concern for other people will force you to make tough decisions. Not everyone is cut out to work in prisons. Some may be unable to cope with the stresses or pay the necessary attention to details. For their sake and the safety of others, you may have to let them go. In doing so, you model responsibility and commitment to the institutional mission.

To build teamwork, leaders must be eager to pull people together, to encourage them to interact and work together collectively to solve problems. Sometimes that means making the process more important than accomplishing the task. Perry Smith, retired Major General, past head of the National War College, and creator of its leadership program, claims that leaders should rarely be problem solvers! Instead, leaders should enable others to solve problems. For the individual, problem solving enhances self-esteem, self-confidence, and ability. Group problem solving builds solidarity and camaraderie. Smith quotes General George Patton saying, "Never tell people how to do things. Tell them what to do and they will surprise you with their ingenuity."[14]

Leaders should never rely solely on a single style. There are times when leaders must be decisive. Swift, unilateral decisions are necessary when the institution is in trouble. These are times when the affairs of the facility need to be managed in minute detail and control is of utmost importance. But, if you want your people to feel personal responsibility for the unit, division, or facility, to have a deep sense of commitment, and to work as a team, you should use a style that is consultive and consensual. When you seek out their comments and their advice, you make staff feel needed. You let staff know that you value their advice and respect their position within the organization. And, by giving them a say, you allow them some ownership of the decision.

Follow up on your initial session. Tell people that you took their advice and give them credit in public. When you make a decision different from what an individual suggests, tell the person why you chose to go against his or her advice. Once people know that you value what they have to say, then they are much more likely to come forward with information that you may not have known to ask for.

Encourage an Entrepreneurial Spirit

The idea of being entrepreneurial may strike you as inappropriate in a public agency, particularly a prison. But the word "entrepreneurial" means to assume the responsibility and risks for an enterprise. Isn't that exactly what we really want of prison personnel, that they be flexible and able to adapt to unexpected situations and the unique demands posed by inmates, staff, and the community; that they react with enthusiasm, zest, and motivation to solve problems and provide quality incarceration? Don't you want to create a climate in which people put passion, creativity, and excitement into their work. Don't you want a staff who takes the prison's interest to heart? That's what I mean by encouraging an entrepreneurial spirit.

Peter Block, author of *The Empowered Manager*, suggests that the choice between being entrepreneurial or being bureaucratic is a choice between greatness and maintenance, between courage and caution, and between autonomy and dependence.[15] Bureaucracy drives us toward stasis, cautiously maintaining things the way they are, always playing it safe in order to assure control and stability. Preserving order in prisons is, of course, imperative. But never forget what Francis Bacon observed more than 350 years ago: "He who will not apply new remedies must expect new evils; for time is the greatest innovator."[16] Just when you think the joint's tied down, the inmates will find new ways to get themselves out or drugs in, the governor will take 5 percent of your staff away, or the teamsters will strike and no one will drive a truck filled with raw vegetables and meat into the facility.

To encourage an entrepreneurial spirit in your people:

1.   Let them know that their survival is in their own hands, not the state house's, not the central office's, not the courts', and not your hands alone. They are free to seek greatness.

2.   Establish an underlying vision of what constitutes high quality incarceration, what conditions will be met and maintained,

what services will be provided, and how people will be treated.

3. Get their commitment to achieving that vision, now. Encourage them to make demands of themselves. People do not take risks out of duty or sacrifice. They take risks because they are deeply committed to the cause and the people involved in it.[17]

Be forewarned. Encouraging an entrepreneurial spirit is to discourage passive behavior among your staff. In fact, you should actively confront passive behavior of your followers. But get ready; that means that they will be honest and even critical about your ideas and actions. They will expect you to respect their ideas and to act on them. They will expect change and improvement and will not be satisfied if you always want to proceed cautiously.

If you are inclined to be an entrepreneurial leader, then there are several characteristics that you will need. First, you will need to be self-confident and self-assured. You must forsake your need for others' approval for the satisfaction of achieving what you believe in—the delivery of high quality incarceration. You will need a strong sense of personal responsibility for achieving that goal.

An entrepreneurial leader needs to be curious—to nose around and find out what's really going on, to question why things are done the way they are, and to experiment to see if new approaches will work better. You have to be willing to take risks even though the bureaucratic tendencies of large-scale organizations resist change. As an entrepreneur, you must confront that resistance directly and press for new (and unproven) ways of doing things. Given this organizational resistance to change, you will need unwarranted optimism at times that you really can make a difference.

Prison systems are steeped in customs, procedures, and enshrined ways of doing things. Given their mission, there are reasons to resist change that may upset their internal order. By chipping away at unnecessary rules and regulations and refocusing on the mission of providing high quality incarceration, you may free the people you lead to accomplish extraordinary things.

PART TWO

PRISONERS

It is the responsibility of corrections to provide a decent, safe, and humane environment and offer opportunities that society may not have provided before then to help some of its misfits improve their prospects for future success in the community.[1]
-- J. Michael Quinlan, Former Director, Federal Bureau of Prisons

It has long been held that criminals deserve to suffer for the harms they inflict on others. The methods for seeing that criminal offenders suffer have varied considerably over time, but generally the historical progression has been toward less brutal punishments that fit the original act. Within this progression, incarceration arrived on the scene relatively recently. The idea behind it is that the loss of liberty over time is sufficiently painful to pay back the harm and right the scales of justice. Prisons, therefore, exist to facilitate the loss of freedom for those individuals convicted of violating criminal laws.

The solitary purpose of denying freedom seems simple enough, but the reality is far more complex. Few people today would seriously regard years of solitary confinement or silent congregate labor as anything except torture. Brutal corporal punishment is not only considered unacceptable in prisons, but officials can be held civilly liable for such acts. Yet, these actions were once commonly practiced in the administration of prisons. Today, prisons still exist to punish, but the suffering they inflict is, and should be, bounded within well-defined limits.[2]

Two factors both define and confound how prisons go about denying the freedom of convicted criminals. The first issue is one of how much suffering an offender should sustain. Is the loss of freedom sufficient, or should the individual suffer greater torment? The trend in this country decidedly has been toward eliminating brutal handling, psychological abuse, hard labor, and unsanitary and inhumane conditions, favoring a position that the loss of freedom in itself is the punishment for criminal offense. This is the proper way to manage prisons. As Mr. Quinlan states in the opening quotation, prisons should be decent, safe, and humane.

The second issue that defines how the denial of freedom gets practiced involves the extent to which prisons attempt to reform criminals. At one end of the spectrum falls the position that prisons have no responsibility for changing criminals. From this perspective, institutions should function to warehouse individuals in order to promote just deserts and to control crime. Alternatively, some argue that rehabilitation serves as the overriding mission of prisons. The position taken by Mr. Quinlan in the opening quotation resides somewhere between these two extremes, that prisons should provide the opportunities for individual change and growth.

Up until the mid-1970s, many prison officials defined the official purpose of their institutions in terms of rehabilitation. For a variety of reasons, the idea of rehabilitation fell into disfavor in the 1970s, leaving many officials in a quandary as to how to articulate their mission.

Many individuals who end up in our prisons derive less benefit from their citizenship than most Americans do. They operate at the margins of society—receiving public assistance, working irregularly in low paid jobs, and participating in illegal activities. Many convicted criminals have long lists of failures in their lives: failure in school, in their families, their jobs, and finally at crime (they got caught!). By harming others, criminals fail to fulfill their social responsibilities as citizens to respect the safety and property of others. John Conrad's idea that prisons should serve as a model for citizenship for such individuals strikes me as an appropriate purpose for prisons to pursue.[3] Otherwise, it seems a bit hypocritical to expect prisoners who have been treated uncivilly to go out and act civilly upon their release from incarceration.

Based upon his experience, Superintendent Lyndon Nelmes of the Guelph Correctional Centre in Canada makes the following observation: "I believe inmates are more likely to exercise good citizenship while incarcerated if they perceive that staff generally perform their duties in a lawful, respectful, intelligent, effective manner."[4]

Conrad argues that as citizens, prisoners possess several fundamental rights for which prisons have an obligation to provide:

1. *"The right to personal safety."* Prisons should strive to protect inmates from physical harm by providing protection, custody, and a safe work and living environment.

2. *"The right to care."* Because they are incarcerated and cannot provide for themselves, inmates should be provided decent,

sanitary housing, a nutritious diet, sufficient clothing, medical care, and recreation.

3. *"The right to personal dignity."* Humanity dictates that all people be afforded self-respect and a sense of personal worth. Beyond the humiliation of incarceration, prisons and their staff should not inflict further indignities or abuse upon inmates.

4. *"The right to work."* Forced idleness can be debilitating and demoralizing to the point of being oppressive. The opportunity to work affords one dignity and worth as a person.

5. *"The right to self-improvement."* Coerced rehabilitation failed legally, penologically, and perhaps morally. However, the denial of the opportunity for self-improvement would constitute a repudiation of hope.

6. *"The right to a future."* Not only do prisoners have the right to self-improvement, but they also deserve a future. For most inmates, this right includes preparation for their eventual return to the community. But for all individuals incarcerated, the right to a future includes the ability to contact and maintain ties with family, friends, and the broader community.[5]

I particularly like the application of the concept of citizenship to how inmates should be treated because citizenship implies reciprocity. To enjoy the rights of safety, care, personal dignity, work, self-improvement, and a future orientation, inmates must act responsibly and fulfill their obligations. For the prison to be safe, inmates must not increase the threat of violence within the community. Likewise, for inmates to enjoy the right of personal dignity, they must refrain from verbal abuse and aspersion of one another.

During the reign of rehabilitation, staff often excused inmates for their disruptive behavior, perceiving the individuals to be sick, disturbed, or in some way incapable of controlling their actions. Such a perspective was consistent with a belief that inmates needed to be reformed. Citizenship, on the other hand, dictates that inmate control is a shared responsibility with the burden of accountability shifted back to inmates: "This is your home and we are going to hold you responsible for your behavior." One correctional administrator described rehabilitation as being like grade school. Control rests with the teacher. Kids act out to test the teacher's authority. In moving away from rehabilitation, prison personnel should now require that inmates act appropriately.

The three chapters of Part III deal with how to handle inmates properly and effectively. I believe that most inmates can be treated as citizens and can be expected to uphold their part of the bargain. Chapter 7 focuses on the first three rights discussed above about how to treat inmates decently. Chapter 8 considers the last three rights concerning how to keep inmates properly involved and with a forward looking perspective. The goal in pursuing these objectives is to provide safe, humane, and productive prisons.

Most prisons executives agree that about 10 percent (or fewer) of the inmates cause about 90 percent (or more) of the problems in institutions. The concept of citizenship has less meaning for these individuals and will not always be useful. Colloquially called the "bad and the mad," disturbed and disruptive inmates have distinctive life histories and institutional lifestyles that require special treatment. Chapter 9 addresses how to handle these particularly troublesome inmates.

7

SAFETY, CARE, DIGNITY AND RESPECT

We must acknowledge that prisons contain a lot of people morally prepared and by experience equipped to take advantage of opportunities to dominate, oppress, and exploit others. The problem of the prison—to construct a system of governance that reconciles freedom with order and security is also the problem of civil society.
-- Albert Cohen, "Prison Violence"[1]

Many of those same individuals who dominate, oppress, and exploit others are, because of their personal histories of failure and mistreatment, easily offended, and they often react quickly with hostility to the slightest affront. Working with these people creates a complex and trying job for prison staff. For prisons to be safe, staff must maintain control. But equally important, staff must respect the fragile, and not so fragile, egos of inmates. Reconciling these two demands requires patience, administrative support, and often considerable training.

Safety
As noted throughout this book, the traditional way of running a prison handled the dual problems of safety and staff/inmate relations through highly autocratic procedures. Discipline was enforced at all levels, and staff and inmate interactions were kept

to a minimum. In many prisons, staff walked the center of the hallways and inmates walked along the sides. Conversations were forbidden, staff strictly enforced explicit rules, and violence simply was not tolerated.

Walpole State Prison in Massachusetts operated this way until a number of factors changed in the 1970s. Inmates pressed for reform, organizing with the support of outside groups and by using the federal courts. In concession to the National Prisoners' Rights Association, policies that had once been used to maintain control were revoked. Simultaneously, inmates changed, becoming more anti-authoritarian and rebellious. The flow of drugs into prison increased, with concomitant increases in turmoil created by the illegal trade of drugs within the underground inmate economy. These modifications in institutional life took place at a time when the rubric of prison reform led to greater permissiveness. Walpole, like so many other prisons, ended up a dangerous place, averaging a violent death every 39 days. The staff countered the turmoil with shakedowns and lockups but were never able to regain control. They feared for their lives and often refused to enter dangerous sections of the institution.[2]

Walpole experienced three problems at the time: (1) ineffective control over staff and inmates, (2) feuding between treatment and custody staff, and (3) labor problems with occasional work stoppages and strikes. Periods of administrative leniency were followed by conservative crackdowns; so no one was clear about policy and procedures. A National Institute of Corrections report described the situation as one in which, "Management has been in a defensive role, putting out brush fires and pursuing a policy of containment."[3] Lengthy lockdowns resulted in inmates abusing staff, verbally insulting and throwing food, feces, and urine at officers.[4]

Control of the Walpole prison was regained in the 1980s. It began with the installation of a new chief executive who did not believe that the violence, budget overruns, and poor morale were in the best interests of staff, inmates, or the citizens of Massachusetts. The new Commissioner set out a long-term strategy for order, safety, and institutional maintenance which included clearly articulated policy and expectations of accountability for both staff and inmates. An effective classification system was established which allowed correctional officers a say in inmate placement decisions. Unit management was initiated to increase decision-making parity between custody and non-custody staff, to facilitate shared responsibility and teamwork, and to increase communication. The new executive was visible and available and thus able to identify and respond to problems before they snowballed into full-scale crises.[5]

Inmates have a right to an environment that is free from violence. Rapes, assaults, homicides, and riots occur commonly in prisons that fail to meet this obligation. Generally, in these situations, the prison staff, and the administrative team in particular, has abdicated responsibility for guaranteeing this right and in essence have allowed the inmates to take charge of the institution. When officials yield control to a group of people who have not been socialized to refrain from violence, it is no wonder that the institution ends up being a dangerous place.

The rudimentary elements necessary to provide a safe environment are present in the changes that took place at Walpole. For a prison to be safe, it must have the following:

1. An executive who believes that it is his or her duty to assure that the facility is under control and that staff and inmates are safe from harm.

2. A well-articulated set of policies and expectations for staff and inmates.

3. A system of individual accountability for staff which requires them to be responsible for the safety of inmates. If their performance falls short of satisfactory, they can and should be disciplined.

4. A system of inmate discipline that is fair and consistently administered.

5. An effective classification system that allows the population to be separated, along with the ability to relocate troublesome inmates to another facility.

6. A practice of every staff member taking personal responsibility for controlling particularly troublesome inmates.

Security in prisons can be maintained in two ways: (1) through physical restraint using bars, metal doors, security screening and other hardware features and (2) by staff assuming leadership roles for maintaining security. Both are necessary; however, reliance solely on physical restraint without active staff participation has been demonstrated unsuccessful. Inmates will fill the leadership void, and though they are restrained within the walls of the facility, they will dominate and exploit one another.

The trend in prison administration recently has been toward less reliance on physical constraint and greater dependence on staff.[6] "New generation" facilities have been built for the past decade which incorporate a podular design of self-contained units for 40 inmates and allow for direct supervision of inmates at all times. Units are designed to restrict movement and breaches of security outside, but within the unit most architectural features associated with prisons—bars, metal doors, etc.—are absent. The new facilities rely on the ability of well-trained officers to supervise and control inmates.[7] Research indicates that these units have lower rates of violence and less graffiti and vandalism than do traditionally designed prisons.[8]

However, building a new facility is not necessary to implement the basic concept of barrier-free supervision. The idea is that staff supervise inmates in a way that is direct and personal. To the greatest extent possible, the approach is proactive, handling issues before they become a major problems, responding to inmates' needs, and resolving conflicts. Staff presence makes drug dealing, intimidation, extortion, and physical abuse more difficult. When a problem arises, staff members are there to take decisive action. A well-articulated system of discipline is available.

Given the psychology of the typical inmate population, prisons can expect ongoing and consistent interpersonal problems, attempted breaches of security, and illegal activities. Direct supervision takes these issues as givens and places staff in the position to be the active eyes and ears of the institutional control system. Staff presence within the population produces considerable information about inmate activities and serves as an early warning system, allowing prompt intervention. Staff availability also provides inmates with access to decision-makers and problem-solvers. It also symbolizes that staff are concerned and responsible.

Hans Toch makes an important observation about maintaining security in prisons. Part of the problem is that we incarcerate violent people, but violence can also be a prison product. Toch lists five actions that facilitate violence within an institution:

1. *Providing "pay offs."* The most obvious payoff occurs when the violent offender gets away with the act of aggression because the staff member devalues the victim, is reluctant to intervene out of fear, or simply does not care and is derelict in his or her duties. This reinforces the act for the offender and chips away at staff control of the facility. Aggressive inmates may also reap more subtle rewards such as peer admiration and status from punishment.

2. *Providing immunity or protection.* Some prisons reward aggressive inmates who maintain peace within a unit by over-looking their acts of violence and exploitation. This too shifts control from the staff to the inmates. Sometimes it works, but it under-mines the right to a safe environment and the example of citizenship and responsibility.

3. *Providing opportunities.* By their very nature, prisons seek routine and predictable operations. Consistent physical move-ment and supervision patterns allow inmate aggressors to plan their acts much as a burglar who observes homeowners comings and goings.

4. *Providing temptations, challenges, and provocations.* If inmates have nothing else, they have time. Idleness provides the first requisite for aggressive inmates to violate others. Next, comes access to weaker or rival inmates, followed by opportunity from lack of surveillance. Tolerating drug dealing and trafficking in contraband, lending, the presence of gangs, homosexual solicita-tion, and racketeering inevitably leads to violence to resolve conflicts.

5. *Providing justificatory premises.* Participation in the dehumanizing and degradation of single inmates and aggregate groups by the staff provides the excuse and provocation for stronger inmates to victimize weaker inmates similarly.[9]

Understanding the causes of violent behavior and devising solutions is a complex and far-from-exact science. A more effective model for attempting to understand and correct the causal factors associated with violence in prison may be to take an epidemiological approach much like the Centers for Disease Control takes with illness. Identify areas of high incidence and target those areas for high surveillance and aggressive intervention. Keep monitoring violent patterns as intensive supervision prompts inmates to shift locations. Also identify low-violence settings which can serve as havens for high-risk victims. Match people with settings to create "safe" mixes of inmate types.[10]

Control of inmates rests on three procedural components: (1) a formal classification system, (2) a well-articulated disciplinary process, and (3) an inmate grievance procedure.[11] A predictive classification model that identifies inmates likely to attempt escape, exploit other inmates, disrupt institutional operations, and assault staff or other inmates will assist staff in segregating the population appropriately. This initial classification should then be supplemented with information about enemies, gang alliances, racist and militant affiliations, syndicate and racketeering connections, and willingness of inmates to serve as informants.

Legally and administratively, prisons need well-articulated and consistently applied disciplinary processes. Most systems use two levels of intervention: (1) *minor*, resulting in a verbal reprimand or formal warning and (2) *major*, where the inmate is formally cited and must go before a disciplinary board. Formal policy outlines precise punishments for specific infractions. It is important for staff not to hide behind formal procedures, but to handle problems with inmates up front and personally, and to attempt to resolve problems informally when appropriate before initiating formal procedures.[12]

The final element of a formal disciplinary system is an inmate grievance procedure. A disciplinary policy assures inmate accountability; an inmate grievance policy in which inmates can question improper, biased, or discriminatory use of the disciplinary system, can allege staff abuse (emotional, psychological, or physical), and can ask for a review of punitive sanctions assures staff accountability. Such review gives inmates formal access to mid- and upper-level administrators and ensures that inmates get a hearing and written reply to their grievances. The process can provide inmates with relief to a broad range of breaches of institutional policy, procedures, and programs. It encourages conversation and conflict resolution, giving inmates an alternative to hostile expressions of frustration and injustice. The system provides prison executives with an indication of professional performance among their staff.[13]

Staff use of violence varies from prison system to prison system. After serving as a correctional officer in a Texas state maximum-security facility, James Marquart made the following observation: "Informal norms of the guard staff justified violence.... The use of unofficial force was so common in the institution. . . that the guards viewed it as an everyday operating procedure and legitimized its use."[14] In contrast, Mark Fleisher observed from his staff role at Lompoc Federal Penitentiary that, "correctional officers' physical and verbal abuse was not tolerated by the administration, the senior correctional staff, the Federal Bureau of Prisons, or the inmates." In place of violence, staff used a variety of styles of talking to inmates as the primary means of control.[15] The success of the federal prison system in maintaining control in light of its policy against the use of violence signifies the viability of the policy. If prisons are to be run as schools of citizenship, such policy is essential.

Ultimately, the success of a prison's control over inmates and the maintenance of a safe environment rests upon keeping inmates busy and not disgruntled. A mix of work, programming, and recreation keeps inmates from having the time to plan and execute exploitative, predatory, and vicious acts. Generally, these activities also assure staff presence to maintain surveillance and to resolve conflicts.

Keeping inmates from becoming disgruntled also helps maintain a healthy prison environment. This does not mean "coddling" inmates, but respecting their opinions. Work to manage their frustrations and assist them in resolving conflicts. Inmates have histories of trouble in these areas. Simply expecting them to function maturely and civilly will not always suffice. It is much the same situation with college professors who expect students to write well. If students arrive at college deficient in writing skills, a professor can either flunk the students who write poorly or can attempt to help them write better. Providing the necessary assistance and encouragement seems appropriate with both groups: students should be taught to write and inmates helped to control their frustrations and resolve their conflicts.

Care

Prisons by design are mundane, routine, and monotonous. This is what it means to lose one's freedom. Many of the people who end up in prison have been neglected throughout their lives. Their emotional needs, education, socialization, dental and medical care, and moral development have not been adequately attended to by either parents or social agencies. So in prisons, many of the little things that staff can do for inmates make a big difference—breaking the tedium of the prison routine, being sensitive, and providing necessary care.

This position is far from universally accepted, particularly among the general public and especially among law enforcement personnel. Some critics argue that inmates, because of the atrocity of their crimes, deserve nothing and should be treated in a mean-spirited, punitive manner. I reject this position on legal and moral grounds, but, equally important, I reject this position because it creates a difficult prison to administer. Adequately cared for prisoners are simply easier to manage.

A second position, perhaps more common among prison staff, is that inmates must earn proper treatment and respect. Like-wise, I reject this position for legal and moral reasons, but also refuse to accept the idea simply because of unlikelihood of its successful fulfillment. Too many inmates are belligerent, hostile, and resistant. A prison system is better off beginning with the premise that all inmates deserve a decent standard of care, which includes dental and health care, tasty and nutritious meals, a certain amount of privacy and other privileges, and the respect of staff. Such humaneness allows the individual personal dignity and establishes a social contract in which the inmate is afforded a decent standard of life and in return is expected to act in a civil manner.

Prisons have a moral and legal obligation to provide adequate health care—medical and dental—for inmates, yet this requirement for most prison executives is an albatross. From years of neglect, poor nutrition, and substance abuse, many inmates arrive at prison with substantial health care problems; consequently, a high demand based upon real needs exists. The situation is complicated by inmates who report for sick call for a variety of non-health reasons: to get out of work, to find sanctuary, or to get attention. Initial and costly triage must be performed to determine medical needs. Health care costs have risen steadily throughout the nation, and prisons have not been immune to this trend with health care consuming larger and larger portions of the total institutional budget. The difficulty of attracting health care providers into prison employment further confounds the situation. Yet, the courts have been vigilant in demanding that facilities meet this need.[16]

It has been said that an army travels on its stomach; the same is true for prisons. Quality food services are essential to high inmate morale and require diligence to maintain. The road to quality begins with balancing cost containment with the purchase of good, if not choice, products. It requires a food service manager who can meet the tastes of a diverse population—from a sizable group that prefers a diet that frequently includes red meat to another large group that eats no pork (the less expensive red meat), Mexicans who prefer spicy foods and Cubans who hate spicy foods, and a growing number of inmates who object to the traditional high starch institutional menus, desiring a healthier cuisine. Even with the purchase of good food stocks and the development of a distinctive menu, quality food service requires a good cook. Presentation is also important. But even this is not enough. When I travel for a week and eat three meals a day in nice restaurants, by the end of the week, no matter how good the food is, I am sick of it. I want a homecooked meal. Inmates respond to prison food similarly; that's one reason they often complain about prison meals. Variety helps. Every so often, offering a special food—brownies, for example, or having a pizza party, breaks the routine. An executive needs to listen to inmate complaints while being attentive to what's going on in food services to make reasonable assessments about quality.

In attempting to provide a decent place to live, prisons also owe inmates a clean and sanitary setting. When Michael Fair became Commissioner of Corrections in Massachusetts, he set out to clean up Walpole. This action soon brought him into conflict with correctional officers who felt that inmates should clean up their own mess. The Commissioner prevailed, and the institution was cleaned.[17] Sanitation demands constant diligence to the task and is an area that is highly sensitive to standards. Over time, sanitation tends to fall to the lowest level of expectation.

A final element in affording quality care to inmates involves the provision of privacy and self-determination. Research concerning inmates' reactions to physical features within the prison setting consistently indicate that environments in which inmates possess some degree of personal control facilitate positive adjustment. Being able to choose to where to spend time, personalize one's private space, and control small conveniences such as ventilation or lighting indicates that inmates' needs for choice and control are respected within the limitations of the prison context.[18] The new generation facilities mentioned earlier are designed specifically to meet these needs by providing greater choice and privacy within highly secure units. Violence, vandalism, and other behavioral problems occur less frequently in these facilities.

Still, allowing as much privacy and self-determination as possible is a tough proviso to realize because the quest of staff to maintain control works in direct opposition to it. The compromise to these conflicting needs may be found in the same principles we articulated for controlling staff: tight but loose principles of management. On one hand, there must be a few ironclad rules for inmates: (1) no shouting or horseplay, (2) regular attendance at work and school, (3) maintenance of clean and tidy personal space, (4) absolutely no exploitative or assaultive behavior, and (5) no possession or trafficking of contraband. Beyond these few regulations, inmates should be given as much freedom of choice as possible within the particular security designation (obviously, maximum security facilities allow fewer opportunities for personal choice than less secure facilities).

Assuring high quality care—including adequate health care, tasty and nutritious meals, and clean and sanitary facilities—requires the same dogged attention to detail discussed in Chapter

2. All the same principles apply. You have to get out into facility and manage by "walking and talking." Inspect everything. Give people the freedom and support to get the job done, but hold them accountable. And most importantly, make your approach corrective, not punitive.

Dignity and Respect

A study asked inmates what personal attributes they found particularly desirable in staff members. With surprising unanimity, the subjects stressed "friendliness and fairness ... rather than permissiveness or leniency." Staff cited as effective took personal interest in inmates and treated them without "pretension or condescension." The staff members were described as "frank, fair, and considerate."[19]

These findings should not be shocking. Inmates all have histories of failure and rejection, and the very act of their incarceration suggests their unworthiness. Consequently, many inmates are particularly sensitive to the slightest gesture of disrespect. Hostile, superior, condescending, and rejecting attitudes by staff will be taken as an attack on the individual's self-esteem and will engender resentment toward the staff and the values they represent.[20]

Most inmates do not want to be incarcerated. They have little interest in the custody goals or the welfare of correctional officers. Consequently, inmates can be uncooperative, challenging, and belligerent to the authority of their keepers. In the face of such resistance, staff may find it difficult to respect and not offend an inmate's dignity. For this reason, this right must be one of the issues recognized by policy and practice as fundamental to institutional operations. It must be the topic of frequent discussion and a norm that is constantly reinforced. Considerable training must be devoted to the topic to assure that it is integrated into professional practice.

Prison workers have three sources of power. They have *legitimate power* by virtue of their position within an official agency. Inmates obey orders because they recognize the lawful right of prison staff in their official position to issue and enforce rules. Whether they like it or not, the majority of inmates, the majority of the time, respect the legitimate power of staff and comply with the rules. But let's face it, all the people in prison wound up there because at some point in their lives they rejected the legitimacy of formal authority and acted in their own self-interests. It is not unlikely that they will again refuse to recognize the legitimacy of authority, reject the right of correctional staff to give orders, or disobey rules.[21]

When this happens, prison staff traditionally turn to *coercive power* to achieve compliance. Staff punish disobedience and reward conformity. Recent reforms have greatly restrained the use of coercive tactics. One survey of correctional officers in Illinois found that more than 80 percent of the officers believe that inmates have gained so many rights that it is difficult to maintain control of the institutions. Punishments that can be levied have been strictly curtailed, and formal hearings are required before sanctions can be administered. Manipulations of rewards—institutional and job placements, good time, and parole—have also been restricted. Given less discretion, staff have fewer opportunities to coerce compliance.[22]

This leaves *referent power*, or personal authority, as the remaining source of control. Here, inmates comply out of the respect they have for the conduct of the guards. Hepburn suggests that staff "who are fair and even-handed in their relations with prisoners, who fulfill their promises to the prisoners, and who exercise their legitimate authority with impartiality and without malice" gain their respect.[23] So there is not only a moral obligation, but a utilitarian benefit in respecting the dignity of inmates.

Based upon his experience at Lompoc Federal Penitentiary, Fleisher claims that a staff member's only "offensive or defensive weapon" is the skill to avoid trouble with talk. Staff must be able to talk an inmate, even a hostile and aggressive one, into doing what the staff member wants.[24]

Within the stark world of prisons, with all their concrete and steel, their starkness, their machismo, and the occasional outburst of shattering violence, the idea of making benevolence an integral part of the prison routine seems almost absurd. But, the unalterable fact remains that the subjects of incarceration are human beings. No matter what the inmate did to get there, the prison's job is to house that individual in a safe and humane setting, not to punish on top of the loss of freedom. A staff member who once was attacked by an inmate and had his throat slashed attests to this philosophy. Despite what had happened to him, he still maintained that, "You've got to treat these guys like everybody else or you won't be able to work with them. You've got to forget what they've done, but always be aware of what they can do."[25] That requires that staff be tolerant, accepting of differences, and at times sympathetic to the inmate's position.[26]

8

A PRODUCTIVE ENVIRONMENT

Regardless of past failures, unflattering recidivism rates, and changing moods and directions, correctional administrators must continually find ways of creating institutional environments that are not only humane but productive.[1]
-- Lyndon Nelmes, Superintendent, Guelph Correctional Centre, Ontario, Canada

The very nature of incarceration—holding people against their will—yields a tendency toward negativism. The people who end up in prison are often hostile, bitter, and disillusioned. They may be dangerous, foolish, or incompetent. They often oppose and resist the actions of staff, distrust staff, and occasionally abuse or assault staff. In response, staff may become cynical, disenchanted, and indifferent. But, as Superintendent Nelmes points out, correctional leaders must constantly fight this tendency toward negativism because the health of an organization is directly related its ability to influence the people within it.[2]

I am not advocating a return to rehabilitation designed around the medical model. Prisoners should not be sent to prison for treatment, nor should they be forced to participate in treatment programs. Their release should not be tied to someone's judgment of their reform. As noted legal scholar and dean of the law school at the University of Chicago, Norval Morris, points out, the idea of a "coerced cure" is oxymoronic. Linking the promise of early release to individual change so adulterated the entire process that no one was able to discern whether individuals were seriously involved in treatment programming. Besides, emphasizing rehabilitation greatly diminished other prison goals of deterrence, incapacitation, and retribution. It distorted the common sense view of justice for both the prisoner and the public.[3]

Engaging prisoners as patients released them from having to be responsible for their behavior. "Inmates" were not considered capable of choosing or determining their own behavior. To me, a much more appropriate view of prisoners characterizes them as volitional and aspiring human beings[4] who in the past have acted irresponsibly and who may or may not act irresponsibly in the future. However, it is entirely appropriate for prisons to expect prisoners to act responsibly. Prisons then exist to encourage law-abiding behavior. They do so by (1) making every effort to ensure the prisoners and staff perceive the operations of the institution as just (guaranteed by rights one, two and three discussed in the previous chapter) and (2) offering opportunities for productive activities that will facilitate individual change and improve the chances of success within the community. Prisons accomplish the second requisite by assuring the three additional rights of citizenship—to work, to have opportunities for self-improvement, and to look forward to their future. In performing these functions, prisons can be civilized and civilizing places.

Members of the public often question why prisons must provide incarcerated individuals with opportunities for productive activities. But, when prisons operate exclusively as human warehouses, no matter how humane they are, they threaten to undermine a person's spirit.[5] Why bother living if there is no hope?[6] No tomorrow. Prisoners, like the rest of us, need something to live for—whether it is release, a new life, or simply better muscle tone that comes from lifting weights.

In my own research in New York state, I found that increased institutional support for self-advancement and self-improvement is associated with less violence and disruptive behavior and with fewer adjustment problems reported by inmates. Life without some tangible goals and the means to pursue them is extremely stark and devoid of purpose. It causes, if not encourages, individuals to fill that void with illegitimate activities and behaviors. Programming that gives individuals some focus and meaning in their life may not reduce the likelihood of return to prison, but it will reduce problems during incarceration.[7]

In the past, prison programming has been judged primarily by whether it reduced recidivism. A better evaluative criterion might be whether a program helps maintain an atmosphere of dignity and hope while the individual is incarcerated. Programming helps civilize and normalize the situation of confinement.

Work

In his speech to the graduating class of Pace University in 1983, past Chief Justice of the Supreme Court of the United States Warren Burger called for an end to construction of "human warehouses" and for their replacement with "factories with fences," where inmates would receive training, have the opportunity to be engaged in useful and productive labor, and be afforded reasonable compensation for their work. Burger recognized that prison inmates are among "the most maladjusted people" and argued that this kind of program would "replace the sense of hopelessness that is the common lot of prison inmates."[8]

The right of prisoners to work should be clearly recognized. An early study of prison reform recognized that, "Enforced labour may be oppressive, but to withhold it would mean even more hardship to the prisoner."[9] Gordon Hawkins states, "There is no justification whatever—neither legal, moral, economic, or penological—for imposing on the offender, in addition to the deprivation of liberty, compulsory unemployment."[10] Article 23 of the United Nations' Declaration of Human Rights states that "Everyone has the right to work, to free choice of employment, to just and favorable conditions of work and to protection against unemployment."[11] Incarceration may pose limitations on this right, but certainly should not revoke an individual's right to work.

Prisons derive at least four benefits from inmate labor. First, it reduces idleness. Inmates when left with little or nothing to do will fill that void with activities of their own, often activities that are prohibited and illegal. In contrast, inmates who work a full day in satisfying jobs are less likely to engage in aggressive and exploitative behaviors, will be less resentful of their situation, and will have less time to organize to resist the authority of staff.[12] A comparison of federal inmates employed by Federal Prison Industries and a control group found that participants displayed better institutional adjustment. The study group was less likely than the controls to have a misconduct reported, and when they did, the incident was less likely to be serious misconduct.[13]

Second, prison labor may provide inmates with valuable training that will prepare them for employment upon release. As Flanagan pointed out in his review of research examining the beneficial effects of prison labor on reforming offenders, the few empirical studies have reached contradictory conclusions: some find a lower recidivism rate for participants while others suggest no differences between participants and controls.[14] However, an extensive longitudinal study of more than 3,000 federal inmates concluded that individuals who participated in work and vocational programming showed better community adjustment. They were less likely to return to prison, more likely to be employed, and earned slightly more than individuals with similar backgrounds who did not participate in such programs.[15]

The third and fourth benefits of inmate labor pertain to cost savings. Using inmate labor for institutional maintenance and services reduces the operating costs of the facility, and the production of goods and services for government agencies may reduce the costs of those items in comparison to free market prices. Yet, both of these benefits have a downside, according to some. Critics argue that inmates involved in institutional maintenance fail to receive valuable work experience that may facilitate their successful reentry into the community. This issue indicates the conflict between the first two benefits. Greater involvement of inmates in a variety of work related programming may reduce idleness but may fail to contribute to the reformative benefits of prison labor.

Critics of prison-made goods and services argue that such practice takes away jobs from law-abiding members of the community and constitutes unfair advantage since prisons are not required to pay free market salaries. Yet, operational and reformative benefits may justify the practice.

In recent years, prisons have experienced renewed interest in inmate labor. This shift resulted partially from the questioning of the validity of the medical model of rehabilitation. If offenders were no longer considered "abnormal" and in need of psychological treatment, then they possibly could benefit from work experience. Furthermore, increasing incarceration rates sent prison officials searching for ways to reduce costs and keep inmates busy. And, finally, renewed interest in the prison labor among the private sector has led to many new joint ventures.[16]

These changes have created the opportunity for prison leaders to be more entrepreneurial in their approach to prison labor. To be entrepreneurial in this case means to be more aggressive and competitive in developing prison industries. It means modeling the "businesslike" practices of free enterprise—developing new products, pursuing new markets, and working more efficiently. It involves paying attention to profit margins and productivity levels.

A manager should recognize that the move to be more entrepreneurial will compete with traditional practices of running an efficient and safe prison. Movement of prisoners within the institution, access to the tools and materials to produce weapons, and congregations of large groups of inmates in industrial areas, threaten institutional security.[17] The conversion of an inmate's status from *prisoner* to *worker* violates the traditional principle of prison administration that says that all inmates should be treated the same. This is because the essence of private enterprise calls for differential reward—pay and other non-wage incentives—to promote productivity. Controlled movement, counts, and lockdowns limit productivity. Industry demands more productive inmates, but security needs the most recalcitrant to be occupied.

A prison leader who becomes more entrepreneurial also risks external resistance, political and legal. Free-world entrepreneurs, especially small business owners, and labor unions will resist prison industries, regarding them as unfair competition. They will lobby legislators to restrict prison industries and may bring civil lawsuits against the state, the system, and the institution.

For a prison executive, the move toward entrepreneurship is not without risks. I happen to believe that the benefits outweigh the costs and that the political environment for such a move is the best it has been in 50 years. Most prison systems have operated small "state-use industries" within their prisons. Their products have consisted of items to be sold to other state agencies and many have enjoyed non-competitive markets. Organizationally, the director of industries has occupied a deputy commissioner level position which placed him or her in a position without considerable power.[18] Within an institution, production has taken a back seat to security considerations. Few incentives promote efficiency or expansion. Industry simply has existed to prevent idleness.

If nothing else, overcrowding has strained the ability of traditional prison industries to employ a significant portion of the population. This has led some systems to be more aggressive in developing prison industries by moving toward a corporate model. This model requires the restructuring of industries to resemble a private corporation. Industry operations are moved outside the correctional structure to stand as quasi-independent entities, retaining their tie to corrections for security reasons, but with a chief executive who reports to a governing board. The model's chief advantage is the increased opportunity for greater capital investment for financing new and existing programs. Operating as quasi-independent entities, prison industries possess borrowing authority similar to other business enterprises. A second advantage is increased purchasing authority resulting from removal of industries from traditional state and prison bureaucracies. Federal Prison Industries, for example, which operates as a quasi-independent entity can buy cotton on the futures market, resulting in a significant cost-savings.[19]

In moving toward business-like operations, prison administrators will want to consider employing managers with private business experience who have the expertise to manage an entrepreneurial enterprise. They may wish to consider other corporate business practices: up-to-date accounting methods, an 8-hour workday, shop-level hiring and firing authority, productivity standards, and an employee incentive system.[20] Many states have found private sector partnerships to be an effective way to bring together the institutions labor force with modern industrial practices and needs.

In balancing the needs of prison industry with those of security, Hal Farrier, former director of the Iowa Department of Corrections, has identified five basic elements that support safe and secure operations. In *locating* an industry, careful consideration must be given to risk posed by the particular enterprise. A proper match with the particular population is needed. A sound *staff development* program will ensure awareness of good security practices. Cross-training of security officers and industry supervisors is critical to an understanding of the demands of both functions. Clearly written, current, and often reviewed *policy and procedures* regarding proper security operations provide the fundamental basis for safe and secure industries. Constant monitoring is essential to assure that staff do not short-cut or compromise practices. Drugs, money, weapons, and messages flow in and out of prisons through industry shipments. Inmates escape, concealed in vehicles carrying industry products. Acute attention to *packaging and product control* is essential. Security is breached far more frequently at the loading dock than the front entrance, yet in most prisons greater attention is given to security of the front entrance. The final element of effective security for industry identified by Farrier is a *positive climate*, where both staff and inmates recognize that lawful behavior is encouraged and is a well-attended to issue. In a safe prison, prisoners have less reason to arm themselves. Where attention to security runs high, inmates recognize the high risks of dealing in contraband. As control deteriorates, problems tend to escalate exponentially as staff energies become taxed.[21]

A word of caution is appropriate here. While in theory, full and productive labor among prisoners is desirable, the road toward that objective is often difficult and riddled with barriers. To be successful, the prison administrator must understand the requirements of running a business operation as well as be able to negotiate difficult political situations within and outside the organization.[22]

Self-Improvement

Why do inmates spend so much time at the weight pile? Part of the reason is that it fills their days. Body building may also aid inmates in avoiding victimization; but, most importantly, lifting weights provides a group of people whose lives have included few successes an opportunity for self-improvement. With weightlifting, a person sees small gains each day. Inmates, perhaps even more so than most of us, need to be provided with opportunities for self-improvement to increase their sense of self-efficacy and accomplishment. This need can best be met by diverse and meaningful programs for self-improvement within the institutional setting.

The "nothing works" philosophy, which was born out of Martinson's conclusions about rehabilitation,[23] left a great many people working in prisons pessimistic, cynical, and wondering what purpose prisons should serve. Ultimately, a belief that "nothing works" can only lead staff to feel that they cannot make a difference in the lives of the men and women whom they supervise; which, in turn, may lead to an attitude of indifference. An indifferent staff can easily let the rights of inmates—to safe and secure settings and lawful and just treatment—slip. Indifference allows staff to justify inappropriate practices and derelictions of duty.[24]

So how did this idea of individual change get so mixed up? In forming the first penitentiaries, the Quakers hoped to achieve "restoration" of individuals by removing them from the corrupting influences of their peers, allowing them time for reflection and self-examination, and providing moral and religious guidance. Over the next 200 years, corrections vastly expanded its approach to reform and moved toward the practice of "coerced rehabilitation" in which freedom was tied to participation in programming.[25] When that practice failed, many prison officials and line staff lost confidence in their ability to influence the lives of their charges and a sense of hopelessness pervaded the environment of their facilities.

The conclusion that "nothing works" misses the point made by critics of rehabilitation. The practice of making reform the purpose of incarceration should have been abandoned. Prisons cannot change someone who does not desire to change. But, prison officials and line staff can create an optimistic outlook and an atmosphere of hope where individuals wishing to change will be supported and have access to the resources to do so. The emphasis then is on providing *opportunities* for inmates to assist themselves.[26]

So what should the specifics of those programs be? Executives will do well to conceptualize inmate needs as falling into three areas: mind, body, and spiritual. The latter two domains, while far from free of controversy (as to what religious practices to permit and how to explain to the public why tax dollars should be spent to provide a wide array of recreational opportunities), tend to be widely recognized and at least minimally provided in all prisons. It is the area of the mind, of changing cognition and judgment, where the most controversy arises.

There are four "must" areas of prison programming aimed at cognition and judgment: education, vocational training, drug and alcohol treatment, and therapeutic programs. Executives should use the following four principles (given in order of priority) to guide the design and implementation of programs:

1. *Maximize participation.* The first priority in putting together a set of programs should be to keep as many inmates actively involved as possible. Evaluate the array of existing and possible programs and the capacity of each. Factor in the duration of the program (e.g., 6 weeks or 6 months). Generally, when making resource decisions, select a program that occupies more inmate hours over a higher quality program that involves considerably fewer hours. Under this principle, even an obsolete program is deemed better than no program at all. The search should be continuous.

2. *Quality programs.* The second priority should be the development of high-quality programs. Program materials should be acquired or developed that are appropriate for adults; technologies should be up-to-date; and most importantly, program activities should be related to successful reentry into the community.

3. *Maximum benefit.* The third priority should be to deliver programs in a way that maximizes benefit. In other words, inmates who would benefit most from particular programs should be

selected for participation. Meeting this condition requires assessment of individual needs and classification based upon program needs. Most programs should have target populations and eligibility requirements. For example, offenders just beginning long sentences would benefit less from vocational training than would individuals nearing release for whom the newly acquired skills would increase their chances of employment in the community.

4. *Efficiency*. Participants should be processed through programs as quickly as can be effectively accomplished. The interests of participants and staff stagnate in programs that move slowly. Inmates may become disruptive and resentful. Consequently, the teaching or training should be facilitated as rapidly as possible, thus keeping the program lively and inmates and staff engaged in it.

By now you probably have realized that these four priorities conflict. Optimizing the number of participants detracts from quality, maximum benefit, and efficiency. What is important is that lower priorities remain priorities and that they get revisited on a regular basis. While trying to increase the amount of time inmates engage in activities, you must try to improve the quality of those programs.

Who could argue that *education* is not an appropriate area of self-development? As the advertisement for black colleges suggests, "a mind is a terrible thing to waste." Many of the men and women who end up in prison have been hampered by their lack of basic reading and conceptual abilities. They have histories of failure in school and suffer the stigma and resentment that accompanies that failure. Increasingly, research links various behavioral disorders to learning disabilities. Consequently, inmates as a group present a population with substantial educational deficits.[27]

Meeting the needs of this group is quite another matter. Diagnosis and treatment of learning disorders is complex and expensive. Adult remedial and learning programs must be different from traditional educational programs designed for children. They require specially trained teachers. Inmates find the classroom materials written for children to be demeaning and insulting. New materials must be written or purchased. Many inmates have short attention spans, little self-discipline, and poor study habits. They lack the motivation to learn. In many prisons, inmates regard assignment to an education program as undesirable.[28]

The provision of quality *vocational training* programs involves similar problems as the provision of educational programs. It is difficult to arrange for vocational training for desirable and sought-after jobs. The public resents the provision of training that will take jobs away from community members, and the provision of state-of-the-art programs is expensive. Consequently, prison vocational training tends to be in fields for which a considerable employment pool already exists—welding, printing, painting, etc.[29] Importantly, researchers have found that having a job upon release does not reduce the chances of return to prison; however, having a satisfying, good job with good wages does reduce the likelihood of return.[30]

Drug and alcohol treatment has shown promising results of reducing recidivism. Douglas Lipton, now director of research for Narcotic and Drug Research, Inc., of New York City, was part of the team that produced what is now often referred to as the "Martinson" conclusion about correctional rehabilitation, that "nothing works." Since then, Lipton conducted a review of drug abuse treatment in prisons for the National Institute on Drug Abuse and has come to a very different conclusion. The results of his study suggest that "reducing drug use and criminality is possible and cost effective." Lipton believes that a comprehensive strategy can lead to a significant reduction in recidivism and drug use relapse among felons who are serious heroin and cocaine drug users. The following five elements must be part of a comprehensive program:

1.   It should concentrate on chronic heroin and cocaine users.

2.   Frequent and systematic use of urine investigation should be employed to reduce drug use.

3.   Therapeutic community drug treatment programs should be initiated within prisons.

4.   In-prison programs must be followed up with treatment in the community.

5. Staff should be rewarded "for creating credible opportunities for inmates to improve."[31]

As with drug and alcohol treatment, there has also been considerable reconsideration of (and debate about) the conclusion that "nothing works" regarding *therapeutic programs*. What appears to be the case is that some programs assist some offenders in not returning to prison. Specifically, it appears that programs targeting chronic, higher risk cases are more likely to succeed than programs that attempt to influence a more general population. Also, programs that focus on the needs which lead offenders to commit crimes show greater promise of success. Specifically, the most favorable targets include: (1) modifying antisocial attitudes, feelings, and peer associations; (2) boosting familial affection; (3) promoting identification with non-criminal role models, (4) enhancing self-control and self-management abilities, and (5) developing prosocial skills to replace lying, stealing, and aggressive practices. Lastly, effectively matching individuals with appropriate programs so that particular needs are met is critical.[32]

Norval Morris makes an important observation about liberating the rehabilitation ideal. Simply providing programs and letting inmates volunteer for them is not enough. To best facilitate individual change, prisons must encourage lawful and positive life inside and outside prison. That is a matter of attitude, of practice, and of environment;[33] which brings us to the final right that inmates have—the right to hope.

Hope

As John Conrad states, "And what more cruel punishment can we devise than to deprive a prisoner of hope that through his efforts or those of someone else his condition may be better in the future than it is at present?"[34] Hope is forward looking. It implies an improved future state of being. For prisoners, that means something other than being held against one's will as punishment for wrongdoing. Hope consists of having a chance, no matter how remote, of living once again as a free person in the community. To deny hope denies promise and aspiration, and ultimately can lead only to a sense of despair and a view that one's life is futile.

Having hope depends on the realization of the other five rights discussed in this and the previous chapter. A future requires the physical safety, mental health, and self-esteem to survive into the future. Building a future also rests upon having the opportunity for meaningful work to gain experience, save money, and gain needed skills. Work helps pass the time. The chance for individual reform and self-improvement allows individuals to prepare themselves for a new life.

Hope also depends on maintaining social bonds with others. For inmates, that includes constructive relationships, devoid of hostility and antagonism, with their keepers. Since there is a natural tendency toward animosity among the incarcerated, maintenance of this principle depends on the staff's professional approach to inmate relations and the scrupulous avoidance of demeaning actions and attitudes toward inmates.

The second aspect in maintaining social bonds consists of allowing contact with community, i.e., family, friends, volunteers, attorneys, and religious leaders. Such relations serve as the bridge to the future and help normalize life in the institution.

To make this happen, a prison must allow inmates to live within the confines of the institution as citizens. According to Robert Johnson, to do so "provides a rehearsal for mature living in the free world."[35] Prisoners without hope cannot be commanded or expected to have a positive view of the future, and in all likelihood without such direction will be unable to constrain their behavior within expected limits. However, it is within the power of prison staff to create an optimistic view.[36]

Quality incarceration will be achieved by (1) imparting respect for the rights of others among staff and inmates, (2) assuring fair and reasonable application of rules and regulations, (3) valuing the lawful and reasonable relationships among people, and (4) providing the opportunity for personal growth in an environment without bias or hostility.[37]

9

DISRUPTIVE AND DISTURBED INMATES

Wherever he went he was always unwanted and unaccepted because of his deep hostility, his strong desire to destroy everything, his unbearable attitude, his immaturity, and his constant and limitless attention-seeking behavior for his dependency needs.[1]
-- A psychiatrist's description of a young inmate who was in constant conflict with staff and other inmates

Within every prison, one encounters inmates, like the individual just described, who seem to work hard at sabotaging their own best interests and end up making life considerably more difficult for themselves than it should be. This young inmate suffered from extremely low self-esteem; he needed the confirmation and affection of others to feel good about himself and to sustain what little positive self-respect he maintained. Yet, to protect himself from the anticipated rejection of others, he acted out with hostility, thereby assuring the exact reaction he expected, rejection, with the consequent result of loss of needed confirmation and affection. Through his own reactions to others, this young man preserved a vicious self-fulfilling pattern of disapproval.[2]

Another self-defeating behavioral response commonly observed among prisoners is that of consistently and defiantly rejecting the authority of staff. The act of denying someone freedom may engender resentment; this is to be expected. Further, an inappropriate or unfair decision by staff may produce legitimate alienation and anger. But, some inmates maintain a posture that staff have no right to tell them what to do. When an officer issues an order, these individuals respond with indignation and outrage. When officers threaten sanctions, the conflict escalates quickly and unreasonably. Such individuals perceive themselves to be exempt from blame. When caught violating a rule, they feel that their infraction should be ignored and that their self-exonerating lies should be believed.

Every official action—request, order, or sanction—becomes a personal affront. For these inmates, staff actions place them in a childlike role that threatens their status as adults. Consequently, as in the previous example, the behavior of these individuals is self-perpetuating. Their adverse reaction to authority invites further direction and enforcement, generating greater defiance by the inmate, and thus the problem tends to escalate.[3]

In the introduction to this section and the two previous chapters, I advocated a model of citizenship to govern the treatment of inmates. Under this plan, inmates are assumed to have absolute rights to safety, care, personal dignity, work self-improvement, and a future. The provision of these rights carries with it the complementary obligation for inmates to act responsibly and to fulfill their obligations. When they fail in these two regards, they are held responsible for their actions, and a well-articulated and fair system of inmate discipline is put into motion. However, for the two types of inmates just described, such a procedure will not effectively alter or control their misconduct. Because they lack reflective reasoning and often fail to consider the consequences of their behaviors, they may not be deterred by punishments. Furthermore, many such individuals lack any sense of reciprocity. They feel that their behavior should go unregulated, and they resent any interference by others.

These inmates are distinguished both by the chronicity of their disruptiveness and by their emotional disorder. One study which surveyed the prevalence of disorder among inmates incarcerated in state, military, and federal prisons found that seriously emotionally disturbed inmates composed between seven and ten percent of the incarcerated populations. Disturbed inmates in the state prison had disciplinary infractions rates seven and a half times greater than the general inmate population; disturbed prisoners in the military facility received six times as many disciplinary reports as the general inmate population, and the disturbed federal inmates' rate was nearly double that of the general population.[4]

Another study identified a group of chronically disruptive inmates who composed only 3 percent of a state prison system sample, but accounted for 12 percent of the disciplinary offenses, 13 percent of the keeplock time served, and 9 percent of time in special housing. These chronically troublesome individuals proved unresponsive to traditional disciplinary approaches, occupied a substantial portion of the disciplinary committees' time, and frequently required placement in high-security settings.[5]

The deinstitutionalization movement, which swelled the numbers of mentally disturbed individuals within the general community throughout the United States, has equally affected the distribution of mentally ill persons in prisons. Court decisions have closed many specialized facilities and have restricted the criteria and tightened the procedures for inpatient placement. As a consequence, few inmates are being hospitalized, and those who are have drastically shortened lengths of stay. The result has been an increase in the numbers of inmates within the general prison population suffering severe mental disorders. These individuals are referred to as "disturbed-disruptive."

The remainder of this chapter explores the patterns of misbehavior among prison inmates in general and discusses how the adjustment patterns of disturbed-disruptive inmates differ from the norm. The characteristics of disturbed-disruptive inmates are described, along with ways to respond appropriately to them.

Prison Misbehavior

It is important to begin a discussion of prison misbehavior by recognizing that most inmates manage to remain fairly trouble-free while serving their sentences. They seldom are cited for rule violations, and few are subjected to formal disciplinary actions.[6]

Like criminal behavior within the community, rule violations within prisons are associated with a few key variables: age, lifestyle, and institutional experience. Younger inmates are more likely to commit infractions than older inmates. Individuals who lived less stable and less connected lifestyles before incarceration (were unemployed, had no high school education, and were not married) are more likely to be implicated in disciplinary actions, along with inmates who had been involved in the criminal justice system and had institutional experiences prior to their current incarceration. It is the young, streetwise, and predatory individuals who pose the greatest threat.[7]

It is exactly this group for which the citizenship model is appropriate and may help successfully control and alter their behavior on a long-term basis. Inmates are treated with respect, offered opportunities, and held accountable for their behavior. A clearly stated set of policy and procedures, consistently applied, provides the needed structure and discipline often lacking in the lives of these individuals.

Research indicates that the behavior of most inmates improves as they proceed through their institutional careers. Rates of disciplinary infractions rise sharply during the initial months of incarceration, then fall quickly as individuals better adapt to their new environment. Infraction rates tend to continue to decline until the individual is eventually released to the community.[8] Not only does the behavior of inmates improve as they progress through their sentences, but, despite a long-held belief to the contrary, their emotional states and health also improve over time. Little evidence suggests pronounced psychological deterioration associated with length of sentence.[9]

It is understandable and predictable that some inmates will experience initial distress upon their incarceration. In many cases, this emotional disturbance will be manifested as non-compliant and aggressive behavior. But, importantly, most inmates adapt relatively quickly to their confines. Of course, some continue to break prison rules from time to time; this is to be expected of individuals with long histories of offense and who have learned to solve interpersonal problems with violence.

However, some inmates will show maladaptive behavioral patterns early in their imprisonment and will maintain these patterns long into their sentences. It is these maladaptive individuals who are of special concern and who require exceptional interventions. Their behavior is the most difficult to manage, and they pose the greatest threat to the safety of staff, other inmates, and themselves.

Characteristics of the Disturbed-Disruptive Inmate

Disturbed-disruptive inmates are often referred to as the "mad and bad." They are troubled inmates who react to stressors in various but consistently inappropriate ways. These individuals are identified at the confluence of the disciplinary and mental health processes within prisons. Because two different types of professionals, who have decidedly different objectives, make decisions about which inmates are both "mad" and "bad," the classification process to identify who is disturbed and disruptive is less than exact. In fact, within many prisons some degree of professional discord exists between the two groups: correctional service officials occasionally feel that mental health professionals fail to properly designate and treat particularly bothersome, hostile, and recalcitrant inmates who could benefit from mental health services; likewise, prison mental health providers sometimes feel that correctional staff inappropriately construe disruptive behavior to be indicative of emotional disturbance.[10]

Two key elements characterize the maladaptiveness of disturbed-disruptive inmates: (1) for a variety of reasons, these individuals do not perceive prison rules as constraints within which they must operate, and (2) their choice to defy, avoid, or disregard prison rules attracts unwanted official reactions which intensifies the situation with which the inmates already cannot cope.

Hans Toch and Kenneth Adams, specialists in prison mental health, conducted the most extensive survey of disturbed-disruptive inmates to date, identifying five maladaptive patterns characteristic of disturbed-disruptive inmates:

1. *Impulse Gratification.* Inmates who engage in this pattern of behavior attempt to satisfy their own immediate or short-term needs with little or no regard for the effect of their behavior on

others. They may use violence or intimidation to get what they want and, when frustrated in their own self-serving actions, they may explode aggressively or act out in blind anger. They seldom engage in necessary reflective assessments that would assist them in learning to satisfy their own needs within a social context; rather they maintain a pattern of childlike actions to fulfill their needs, which results in adverse reactions of staff and other inmates.

2. *Esteem Enhancement.* In another common maladaptive approach, inmates attempt to maintain their own self-esteem through exploitative or destructive behavior. They may build a self-image around aggressiveness. When insulted, which happens easily, they respond with hostility or aggression. Because of poor self-images, they may expect to be rejected and lash out with hostility.

3. *Autonomy Pursuit.* Another behavioral response is associated with inmates' relationship with authority and their own self-images as independent adults. One group falling into this category maintains a pattern of dependence on authority figures and unreasonably expects intercessions to assure that their needs are met. At the opposite end of the spectrum are those inmates who consistently defy and challenge authority in their attempts to maintain their autonomy. In either case, the inmates sustain a childlike view of authority responsibilities—authority figures are either there to meet their every need or to be resisted in order to establish independence.

4. *Refuge Seeking.* Most inmates find a niche within the prison community where they feel reasonably safe and comfortable; however, some inmates become vulnerable or perceive themselves as so defenseless that they must seek sanctuary. The stress posed by the threats of other inmates cannot be tolerated. And for some, initial exploitive, aggressive, or socially clumsy behavior places them in a position of needing refuge.

5. *Sanity Maintenance.* For a final group, the struggle to cope with the social surroundings of prison becomes too great, and they lose contact with reality. These inmates tend to withdraw from the social environment of the prison, often refusing to leave their cells even when requested to do so. They neglect personal hygiene and self-care. However, also characteristic are explosive

outbursts and attacks brought on by paranoia and delusions. Self-destructive behavior is common.[11]

What best characterizes disturbed-disruptive inmates is the chronicity of their maladaptation. They engage in misbehavior habitually and repeatedly. Their acts may vary, but their reasons for misbehaving remain consistent.[12]

Management and Treatment of Disturbed-Disruptive Inmates

There are two main aspects to consider when dealing with disturbed-disruptive inmates: what to do when the inmate is acting out, and second, what disciplinary/treatment actions should be taken in response to the incident?

If estimates are accurate and between 7 and 10 percent of most prison populations suffer emotional disorders, then somewhere between 1 in 10 and 1 in 15 inmates are at risk of an emotional disturbance at any time. For this reason, staff should be prepared to handle violent, acting-out inmates as a part of their duties. This feature of prison employment should be clearly recognized. Prisons should be honest with new employees during recruitment and orientation about the incidence of violence.

Importantly, a prison must have a clearly written set of policies and procedures for crisis intervention. These regulations should delineate who has responsibility for what functions. During an incident, security personnel need to be in control of the situation, and one person should be identified by policy, in advance, as the one in charge. However, it may be helpful to use a team approach when possible, involving correctional, unit management, and psychological services personnel.

It is essential that all staff—security, treatment, and support—be trained in crisis intervention procedures and techniques for handling emotionally disturbed behavior. Part of this training should include an understanding of the psychological dynamics of disturbed-disruptive inmates. Staff need to comprehend that these inmates are experiencing panic and anxiety, that they have lost their ability to control their situation and are acting out to relieve feelings of helplessness.

The fundamental goal of intervention should be to gain control of the situation without injury to staff, other inmates, or the individual. Training should emphasize that intervention should involve the *least* necessary force to handle the situation. The aim is to defuse the aggression and violence. Be firm and forceful, but avoid being threatening or demeaning. Staff must be taught to maintain a professional and respectful attitude, remembering that these inmates have extremely fragile egos. Admittedly difficult, staff *must* be encouraged not to view the violent-aggressive inmate as an opponent or as the enemy. Staff responding to the incident should minimize the visual cues that they may be feeling angry or afraid; the approach should be calming and reassuring. Remember that the inmate is frightened and has lost control. Staff must establish that they are in charge and are there to protect themselves, other inmates, and the individual experiencing difficulties.

Hank Cellini, a correctional program specialist for the National Institute of Corrections, has identified seven essential elements for a crisis intervention strategy:

1. *Place one person in charge.* In advance, designate who is in control of the situation. Others who respond to the incident must be trained to know who will assume command and must respond to that individual's orders.

2. *Clear the area.* The goal is to bring order to the situation as calmly as possibly. Remove all bystanders—staff and inmates—from the area. Retain sufficient security personnel at the periphery to restrain the individual if the situation cannot be defused.

3. *Avoid further provocation of the individual.* When a person is frightened or enraged, the body pumps large amounts of adrenalin into the blood system to assist in the "fight or flight" response. In this excited state, violent reactions are easily triggered. Avoid agitating the disturbed individual. Do not threaten or provoke. Refrain from asking what is troubling the person because that will only heighten concern about the traumatic situation.

4. *Acknowledge the individual's anger.* The purpose of this response is to shift the individual's attention away from the traumatic event causing the person to act out and toward the

individual's own behavior and how it is affecting him or her. Be as specific as possible; let the individual know that you can see that he/she is so angry. Acknowledging this anger provides the individual with the option to calm down.

5. *Inform the person that you are in control.* A person in crisis has lost the ability to control his/her own behavior, which results in fear and agitation. Let the individual know that you are there to protect him/her and others. The individual needs to be reassured.

6. *Do not interpret loudness to indicate dangerousness.* The fact that an inmate is shouting does not necessarily mean that the individual is likely to be violent. One does not necessarily lead to the other. However, the exception may be inmates who have been diagnosed with borderline personality disorder. These individuals are guided by inner thoughts and perceptions that are unconnected with reality.

7. *Look for signs of drug abuse.* Bringing an aggressive or violent inmate who is under the influence of drugs under control is substantially more difficult and risky. When responding to a crisis situation, staff must quickly determine, if possible, whether the inmate has recently used drugs.[13]

The purpose of the procedure outlined in these seven steps is to defuse the crisis. In doing so, staff take control of the situation. They clear the area to protect others and to avoid interference. The staff member speaking directly with the inmate tries to calm and reassure the individual that staff are in control and can keep the person from harming himself/herself or others. The response is not threatening or intimidating. In some cases the strategy will not be successful and the individual will proceed quickly from hostility to aggression. At this point, staff must act swiftly to restrain the inmate and prevent further violence. Training and practice in crisis intervention will assure that the approach is carried out as it should be.

After the incident has been brought under control, the question of how to properly respond to the misconduct must be considered. Chronically maladaptive inmates demonstrate through their very behavior that traditional sanctions and punishments will not have the desired deterrent effect on their actions. Some other response is necessary. However, altering a disciplinary process intended to be fair, consistent, and just, runs the risk of defiling the process in the eyes of staff and inmates. What is needed is a procedure that maintains the integrity of the disciplinary process while monitoring and responding to chronic maladaptiveness.

Toch and Adams recommend a two-tiered procedure which preserves the integrity of the disciplinary process to ascertain culpability and establish a disposition. It then augments that procedure with a second process to monitor and respond to chronicity. The purpose of the second procedure is to understand why the individual keeps repeating a pattern of maladaptation and determines how the individual might be assisted in behaving differently. As such, the two-tiered system provides a way to integrate mental health diagnoses and treatment procedures into the disciplinary process. Disciplinary action must be judicious, thereby protecting the due process rights of offenders. The process must focus solely on the instant offense, be handled formally, and provide a sanction that fits the offense.

The second procedure begins with a different set of questions and an altogether different purpose. Rather than considering only the instant offense, the pattern of maladaptation is reviewed in search of explanations and identification of precipitating events. Unlike the disciplinary procedure where the offender is the target of the process, in the second procedure the individual may become a participant. Here the focus is on the future and how to prevent further maladaptation. These procedures can be informal.[14]

The two-tiered process can be implemented nicely within a unit management system. As part of their regular duties, case managers monitor inmate misbehavior for chronicity. When they observe a pattern, a team of correctional personnel, psychologists, and unit staff can be assembled to evaluate the case. The inmate can be invited to the team meeting and questioned about his or her perceptions of the problem and how the individual thinks s/he can be helped to cope. The goal is to alter the circumstances of the inmate to allow the individual other alternatives than maladaptive responses.

Understanding how inmates adapt will assist teams in helping maladaptive inmates find alternative behavioral patterns.

According to Toch and Adams, these inmates "do not undergo marked conversions or reform. They do not become resilient, flexible, competent, or achieve insight, perspective and self-knowledge." Instead, they adapt by trial and error; lacking insight and planning concerning the consequences of their efforts, they proceed chaotically. However, improvements in personal functioning may occur serendipitously. Some circumstances end up being more manageable and more comfortable than others. Inmates find that they can handle the challenges of certain situations better than others.

Prison officials can assist in this process, not by aiding the individual in gaining insight, but through manipulating settings to find a better fit. Maladapters can sometimes benefit from transfers that provide "fresh starts." Placement in less social, lower pressure circumstances may relieve tension that results in disruptive responses. Some maladaptive inmates find that the restrictiveness of punitive settings provides the isolation and/or structure they need to cope. To the extent that the assessment team can understand the specific psychological needs of maladaptive inmates, the more likely it is that an appropriate set of circumstances can be devised.[15]

Conclusions

In Part 3 of this book, I have argued for a citizenship model to guide prison employees in their handling of inmates. Understandably, this requirement will pose a significant challenge for staff and will test their mettle. It is difficult to respect the dignity of individuals who grossly neglect their own personal hygiene. It is hard to come to the aid of persons who, time after time, through their own actions trigger their victimization by others. It is almost impossible to care for individuals who consistently react with hostility and aggression. But if these are fundamental values of the organization, then it is essential that staff adhere to them for *all* inmates.

For staff to be able to do this, they need clear guidelines and considerable training. They also need to be consistently reminded of the importance of the values. This will occur to the extent that prison officials stress the values, monitor for compliance, and take corrective action.

PART THREE

LOOKING TOWARD THE FUTURE

As I look out over the business landscape, I see common patterns of change. These changes are so sweeping that, not surprisingly, many business observers are speaking in terms of a new age.[1]

-- William G. McGowan, Chairman, MCI

The way in which business gets done in our world is changing dramatically. The marketplace is highly unsettled; some sectors are shrinking while new opportunities abound in others. Competition is intense as new competitors vie for a piece of the market. The very foundation of once stable and staid corporations, such as IBM, are being rocked. Companies face deep uncertainties. There was a time when IBM virtually controlled the computer market, dictated technological development, assured its employees of life-long employment, and guaranteed its investors an annual dividend. Many analysts, employees, and investors thought that situation would never change. It did!

In response to a highly unsettled market, companies are changing how they are organized and how they operate—they are becoming more *agile*. Agility implies flexibility and the capability of responding quickly. Traditionally, business organizations were highly structured, with distinct divisions of labor, and centralized control. That structure promoted efficiency, but made organizations sluggish when it came time (or they faced the need) to adapt. In a chaotic and uncertain business environment, traditional structures simply cannot respond quickly enough to changing markets. To be responsive and competitive, businesses have had to be more creative; they have had to anticipate what was going to happen in the market, and develop new products and new ways of doing things. To be creative, they had to decentralize, so that decision-making was pushed down to the personnel closest to the product and the markets. Greater participation became necessary throughout the organization. So companies began to stress openness, teamwork, and a customer orientation.

With the move away from centralized control, companies needed something to hold everything together. Their answer has been the creation of strong organizational cultures with clearly stated sets of values. Whereas, traditional organizational structures treated employees in an impersonal manner, as interchangeable cogs in a machine, decentralized organizations needed individual commitment to an overall mission; they needed for employees to feel a sense of ownership. To get that level of commitment, companies had to treat employees not as mechanistic, interchangeable parts but as integral individuals who were expected to take initiative and responsibility for the operations of the company.

So what does all this about the business world have to do with prison administration? There are "experts" who argue that these changes have no implications for prisons or their operations. These "experts" claim that prisons should *not* change the ways in which they have always conducted their affairs. They argue for a traditional design and management style which includes a paramilitary structure that severely limits discretion for line personnel and concentrates power and decision-making at the top of the organization. I think these "experts" are wrong. I believe that prisons are finding themselves in a chaotic and turbulent situation, just as American businesses are, and that similar pressures for change exist in both prisons and corporations. Furthermore, prisons cannot and will not exist as isolated, unchanging institutions that continue to operate as they always have, while other institutions are changing radically. The way employees are regarded and treated in the private sector has implications for how employees in the public-sector of prison work expect to be treated.

At the heart of the dramatic changes experienced by prison systems during the past decade has been the greatest overall expansion of prison capacity in American history. Simply finding sufficient space for the burgeoning populations has been challenge enough, but creating the physical space has been just the tip of the iceberg. As the number of inmates increased, so did the need for additional staff, creating substantial recruitment and training demands. Accelerated processes associated with rapid growth rendered ineffective the old ways of socializing and integrating new employees to help them assimilate the values, traditions, and methods of handling inmates. Numbers were too great and time was too short.

Rapid growth increased not only the need for entry-level personnel but for mid- and upper-level administrators as well. Here, too, old ways of identifying, grooming, and ultimately promoting qualified individuals no longer worked. Time spent in a position has been greatly compressed. Whereas a decade ago, officers waited (and learned and developed) an average of six to eight years before promotion, now promotions routinely occur within the first two years of prison service. When systems were small, promotions were made by senior personnel who were personally acquainted with the candidates; now, systems are too large for senior administrators to know everyone they promote.

The challenges for prison administers extend far beyond handling this growth in numbers of inmates and staff. Changes in the criminal laws, with determinate sentencing and new drug enforcement acts enacted in many states and the federal government, have altered the characteristics of the inmate population. New admissions to prison are younger than in the past (primarily due to the increasing numbers of young drug offenders), yet with increased lengths of sentences, their average age is actually growing older.

Prison budgets have increased to accommodate the expanding numbers of inmates and staff, although in many cases the increase in fiscal resources has not kept pace with the population growth, and prisons have had to do more with less. Still, the budgets of many prison systems have increased sufficiently so that the corrections agency is among the largest state or federal offices. This change has resulted in greater external scrutiny by the legislature, government budget offices, and the media. No longer so isolated, prisons now must be far more accountable to external groups. Senior-level administrators must now devote substantially more time to dealing with externalities—other agencies, the press, members of Congress, and their communities.

The workforce is also changing. Traditionally, prisons have been a bastion of white males; now, increasing numbers of minorities and women are entering prison service. Predictions indicate that white males will compose an increasingly smaller fraction of available workers to be recruited.

Finally, technology is changing. Electronic perimeter surveillance is less costly and more effective than traditional high walls and "manned" towers. Gates are electronically opened at a central control center rather than by an employee with a key. Computers are becoming commonplace to maintain inmate and staff data systems.

New inmates, new staff, new scrutiny, and new technology— who says there is not tremendous urgency for change in prison administration? However, during turbulent times, it is difficult to think about the future. The greatest temptation for managers is to focus more on doing than on thinking, to react to what is happening now and neglect the long term. Leaders are needed who can manage change in the present, but who can simultaneously redirect organizations so they are prepared for the future. A senior executive in a large international corporation observed, "We will always need senior managers who can lead people in certain directions, but the concepts of leadership are changing. We need a different kind of leadership, in which the leader can generate a sense of vision and purpose, and can create an atmosphere in which other people can share it."[2]

Stanford University professor Harold Leavitt suggests that good management involves "taking hold of complex, messy, ill-defined problems and converting them into organized, systemized forms." To do this, managers must engage in problem solving— analyzing, exercising judgment, and planning—and implementation—doing, changing, and convincing. But Leavitt counsels that lurking behind these two important processes is an activity which he calls "pathfinding." Pathfinding is about finding mission, determining purpose, and developing vision.[3]

Leavitt explains that pathfinding requires intuitive and creative thinking which is different from the day-to-day analytical cognitive processes needed to make decisions within an organization. But, pathfinding also requires the individual to assess his or her own values and principles. Out of those beliefs, a pathfinder can begin to form a *vision* of what could be and to fashion a strategy to realize it. That takes determination and conviction.[4]

I contend that these are exactly the characteristics needed by contemporary prison leaders. We need men and women with strongly held *values* about what staff and inmates deserve in the institutions in which they work and live, who can formulate those beliefs into *visions* of how their organizations should operate, and who have the moral *determination* to see that those lofty ideals are realized.

The final three chapters are about pathfinding. Chapter 10 discusses vision. It is about looking into the future, and it's about intuition and imagination. But, it is also about grounding that creativity in integrity, and about commitment and values. Chapter 11 provides guidelines for implementing vision through strategic planning. This chapter discusses the process but also stresses the importance of linking strategic planning to alternative futures rather than simply documenting present activities. Chapter 12 explores the prison executive's job. It discusses the elements of the job and the traits needed to accomplish those endeavors. The chapter then reflects on how best to develop future leaders who can successfully guide prison systems into the next century.

10

DEVELOPING A VISION

The message for correctional management is clear: We must move beyond the realm of traditional management into creative leadership if we are to deal effectively with our changing world. ...We must create a fresh vision of our shared future and develop leaders who are able to understand the world in which we live today, to see trends as they develop, and to recognize and deal with concerns before they become problems.[1]
-- David C. Evans, former Commissioner, Georgia Department of Corrections

It was with some apprehension that I chose to use the word, *vision*, in this chapter. Prison officials tend to be pragmatic and practical individuals who are decisive and who enjoy working in a world that is tangible and concrete. People in law enforcement and prison work generally appreciate orderliness, are comfortable with rules and regulations, like stability, and are often troubled by change. For some, I suspect the word *"vision"* may be too soft, mystical, or abstract. But, before you reject the concept, I urge you to think about the topic for a moment.

Is your prison or your unit within the prison currently operating to perfection? Is it meeting your standards of excellence? Think about your own values about prisons. How should prisons operate?

What obligations do prison organizations have to their employees? What fundamental rights do prisoners have? What responsibilities do prisons have to the public? What is your personal agenda? How would you change the institution if you could? What do you want to prove?

If you have answers to some or most of these questions, then you have, at the very least, the beginnings of a *vision* for your organization. There is something out there in the future that you want to accomplish; you want to make a difference.

Change in prisons can be threatening. It can result in instability, and instability can lead to the loss of control. Consistency, orderliness, and predictability are what running prisons is all about. Maintaining control is foremost in their missions, but change is inevitable, in prisons as in any organization. Why? Because the world in which prisons operate changes, and this creates pressure to adapt.

In the introduction to this section, I identified seven changes currently taking place in prisons: (1) rapid expansion of inmate populations, (2) increased recruitment and training demands for staffing, (3) accelerated advancement for staff, (4) changes in the characteristics of the inmate population, (5) increased visibility, external scrutiny, and accountability, (6) alterations in the workforce available to be recruited into prison service, and (7) technological advancements. These events produce pressure to which prisons and their officials must adjust.

A good example of external pressure and visionary leadership occurred when Norman Carlson decided to step down as Director of the Federal Bureau of Prisons in 1987. Carlson epitomized the pragmatic prison executive who managed by "walking and talking." He knew the people who worked for him and stayed acutely aware of what was going on in the prisons under his direction. Because of his extensive personal knowledge of the federal prisons' operations, Carlson was able to make good decisions by consulting those around him and coupling what they said with on his own understanding of the situation. He was not an ardent consumer of research or external information; rather, he relied on his own intuition. But, Carlson saw the future. He recognized that the Bureau of Prisons was about to undergo unprecedented growth, and with expansion, the Director would no longer be able to know most everyone under his command, nor would he be able to as closely monitor the operations of each and every prison. So when it came time to recommend his successor, Carlson selected a manager with a truly different style than his own, J. Michael Quinlan. That was visionary leadership. Carlson anticipated change and selected an individual, quite unlike himself, who would be capable of steering the Bureau through its growth and transition.

As it turned out, Quinlan, too, was a visionary leader. He was dedicated to the Bureau's longheld commitment to monitoring operations, managing by walking around, and inspecting everything, but recognized that Bureau was expanding so that at the national level these activities could no longer be conducted by an individual but had to be institutionalized at an organizational level. He expanded the role of the Division of Program Review to ensure that high quality and consistent monitoring would occur throughout the system and that information about prison operations would be available at the national level. In this manner, he and other officials at the national and regional levels could stay well informed of occurrences in the field. Furthermore, he worked with the Office of Research to create a management information system that would provide strategic information from program reviews and other information sources readily, consistently, and reliably to all managers. Quinlan possessed the same values of quality assurance that had always characterized Bureau of Prisons executives, but through his visionary leadership, he reformulated them to fit a rapidly expanding system.

It is important to recognize that in both the examples just given, visionary leadership was exercised to ensure the continuance of those critical values of consistency, orderliness, and predictability in prison operations in the face of considerable pressure for change. So, you see, the idea of being visionary and attempting to maintain stability are not inconsistent practices.

Elements of Vision

Both Carlson and Quinlan formed mental images of the future for the Federal Bureau of Prisons and then translated those images into reality through their actions. That is what developing a vision is all about. The process begins when a leader identifies forces within or outside the organization that may impact and shape its future. The leader anticipates how those forces may be played out and begins to consider how to guide the organization through the transition. This process is cognitive and involves moving from the identification of *possible futures* to the selection of a *preferable future*. The image of the desired future is the vision.[2] When articulated, it becomes a statement of destination.[3]

Kouzes and Posner tell us that there are four elements to visions. First, as the name implies, they are visual; they conjure within us images, mental pictures of what the future could be. Visions, then, are impressions that exist within our minds. They are simply abstractions about possibilities until leaders breath life into them and portray them as concrete images that are within reach. At that point, visions become reference points for all current and future actions.

Second, having a vision assures a future orientation within the organization. For example, at some point in time—next year, in four to six years, at some point in the future—a more desired set of circumstances will exist. As I discussed in Chapter 4, people are happiest when they are challenged, when they have something to work toward; they want to be part of something and to make a difference. People desire leaders who create this type of work environment by being forward looking and formulating a long-term image of something to strive for. Visions provide the medium to keep everyone's attention directed toward the future.

Third, visions focus attention on potential, on an idealized view of a preferred future for the organization. As such, visions shift our thinking from what is probable, to what is possible. Probabilities imply what is likely to occur, but possibilities are not bound by those limitations and, thereby, free our thinking to consider what could be. As such, visions encourage optimism and hope for a better day.

Fourth, visions help define uniqueness. By describing where it is headed, they set the organization apart from all others. They delineate for the people working in the organization as well as those outside it, how this particular group of people is exceptional. By setting a standard, visions become sources of identity for the organization itself as well as the people who work within it.[4]

What then is a vision? Kouzes and Posner define it as *"an ideal and unique image of the future."*[5] A vision often begins as a vague dream of what you would like to accomplish. Your desire to achieve something then forces you to clarify the dream within your mind. You begin to formulate an image of what your organization or unit could be. As the dream becomes clearer, your determination to work toward it grows. It takes on new intensity, and you can no longer keep it to yourself. Increasing fervor forces you to enlist others to accompany you in this journey.[6]

So, you see, there are a number of elements in the formulation of visions. The process begins with imagination and creativity, takes on emotion and passion, and finally leads to the solicitation and involvement of others. Yet, as I have already mentioned, the people who end up working in corrections tend to prefer stability and resist change. These individual characteristics may inhibit the processes of imagination and creativity. Furthermore, aspects of prison work itself may suppress these processes. It is easier to be innovative in situations where there are no rules than in situations, such as in prisons, with rigid constraints. Some professions—architecture, for example—encourage creativity. An architect is expected to produce original ideas. But, prison professionals are encouraged to conform, to keep the institution on a steady keel. Compliant and convergent thinking is safer than divergent thought.[7] Prison employees need to be logical, clearheaded, and rational, but these attributes may suppress the "dreamer" trait needed to be creative and imaginative. One would hardly wish for a group of prison employees with their heads in the clouds.

If you truly want to be an extraordinary prison leader, you will likely have to overcome some of your own individual tendencies and some organizational barriers. John Gardner probably has provided one of the best guides on how to do this. He says that leaders have to have "positive attitudes toward the future," but must recognize "that life is not easy and that nothing is ever finally safe." Gardner calls this "tough-minded optimism." Leaders must inspire confidence and keep hope alive, but they must also remember that enthusiasm, faith, and aspiration can be dashed when high hopes are thwarted.[8] So the pragmatic orientation of most prison executives may serve them well, if they can periodically escape their preoccupation with doing, and spend some time thinking, dreaming, and conceptualizing, to look beyond the immediate demands of the organization and toward creating an idealized form of the institution that might not suffer some of the problems currently faced.

Getting a Vision

So where do you go to get a vision? Moses went to the top of a mountain and waited for God to speak to him. Native American shamans used peyote to clear their minds and induce a dreamlike trance to prepare themselves for a vision. I recommend neither of these practices for prison executives, but they do provide some guidance in how to get started.

First, *turn to your values*, including your own religious values. Let your god speak to you, because religious principles will guide you in how you should treat your employees and prisoners. They will define for you high standards of practice, integrity, and decency. Your secular and spiritual principles should help inspire a vision of how your organization should be.

Next, *clear your mind* and prepare yourself for developing a vision. Using peyote may not be an acceptable approach, but somehow you must free your mind from the day-to-day operations of the facility, get away from dealing with the probable future, and reflect on what might be possible. That occasionally happens naturally, late at night when you finally relax and your imagination has a chance to engage. It is a good idea to keep a notepad next to your bed so that when those late-night inspirations come, you don't run the risk of forgetting them by morning.

If you do not want to leave inspiration to chance, you have to make time for it and create settings that will nurture your imagination. At a minimum, that requires closing your door and having your calls held, but it may entail getting away from the office altogether. Go someplace inspirational, a scenic location; view something inspirational, a masterpiece of art; or watch something inspirational, the N.B.A. playoffs. And, then contemplate excellence, how it looks and how it feels, and why it is important.

Reflect on your past. Intuition and creativity do not flow from a vacuum, rather they build upon knowledge and experience. Routine clearly inhibits creativity, but people with more knowledge of how things work are better prepared to reconfigure operations in order to produce more desirable results. So think about your experiences in the organization. What works well? What really bothers you? When did extraordinary things get accomplished? Is there too much paperwork? Are there too many layers of bureaucracy? Is there too much gossip and petty politics? Based upon your experiences in the facility, how should things be done differently?[9]

Attend to ideas as they come to you. Take time to jot them down. Mull them over. Meanwhile, monitor what is going on inside and outside the organization. What pressures bear on the future? What opportunities are beginning to present themselves? How do your ideas fit into the changing world?

Consult with others. Tom Peters suggests scheduling a series of meetings with various groups in the organization: front line staff (correctional officers, teachers, case managers, and secretaries) from every functional area, first-line supervisors, your trusted associates, and community leaders.[10] Get feedback about whether your perspective of the future fits with others' perceptions. Learn from their experiences. Now, discuss your ideas and try to get an open and honest reaction.

Now, *start to clarify and articulate the vision.* See if you can write it down concisely and powerfully. To test its validity, ask yourself, "is this something about which I have a strong personal conviction?"

Peters suggests that when you assume an executive office, you move relatively quickly to articulate a vision of what you will accomplish. The notion of a president's "honeymoon" in national politics is fitting. You have about 100 days to set out what will be achieved during your tenure.[11]

Values and Vision in Prison Work

In the previous section, I suggested that you begin to develop your vision for your prison or unit by reflecting on your own values about how people should be treated. Ultimately, your vision must be your own and must reflect your most deeply held sentiments. Otherwise, it is unlikely that you will possess the necessary commitment and passion to sustain efforts to realize your goals. Neither I, nor anyone else, can tell you what is really important; that must come from within you. However, there are two values about prison work that I think you should consider.

The first is that prisons should be *lawful*.[12] I doubt that anyone who works in a prison reading this statement will disagree. How can the state's strongest action taken against citizens who violate its laws be administered within *lawless* communities? The idea itself seems oxymoronic, but that condition exists in many institutions across the nation. In some cases, the lawless conditions within prisons occur with intent; men and women employed in the institution become corrupt. More often, however, prisons become lawless due to neglect. It is easier to overlook some infractions, not to intervene in the activities of stronger inmates and gangs, and just to keep the lid on things.

Ensuring that prisons are lawful places requires considerable perseverance. First off, for prisons to be lawful, no unlawful conduct by prisoners can be tolerated. Any exception to this rule violates the standard and will serve as notice to staff and prisoners that the principle of lawfulness can and will be compromised, thus totally discrediting the entire issue. This means that staff must be constantly vigilant in enforcing rules and laws. They cannot fail to require rule compliance from stronger inmates and gangs, nor can they overlook infractions in exchange for keeping a unit under control. They must patrol and search for contraband.

For the prison to be lawful, the disciplinary process must also be credible. The demands of due process must be observed. Punishments must be consistently and fairly administered.

To be lawful institutions, steps must not only be taken to ensure compliance among the inmates, but also among staff. This requirement demands diligence among officials to root out corruption and dereliction of duties. Once again, constant surveillance is essential, not only to detect offenses, but to symbolically reinforce the value of lawfulness itself.

Properly administered grievance procedures for both staff and inmates are needed to secure each group's right to express objections, to have those objections taken seriously, and to have actions taken if the complaints are found to be grounded. Grievance procedures extend the process of assuring lawfulness to everyone within the organizations. It is a formal, open, and controlled method of making everyone responsible for seeing that the institution remains lawfully governed, not just left to administrative discretion.

The second value for prison work that I propose you consider in developing your vision is *optimism*. Prison work is hard for all employees. Prisoners resist and even hate you; the public doesn't understand, and certainly doesn't seem to appreciate, the work that you do; and public officials fail to provide you with sufficient resources to accomplish what they expect of you. As a consequence, prisons yield an excellent breeding ground for pessimism. You have seen it—that unflagging cynicism among your peers; that sense of hopelessness, defeat, and failure; the loss of enthusiasm.

With pessimism comes a sense of powerlessness and unconnectedness to the events and activities of the organization. Employees do not feel that they can change things or improve them. They put in their time, but coming to work is essentially unpleasant. Bureaucratic defensiveness surfaces as an excuse for never improving operations, and rigidity sets in throughout the agency.[13]

Leaders can do something about pessimism. Through vision, they create a positive view of the future. They provide their employees with something to work toward, a challenge. A major element of the vision must be keeping hope alive.

Enlisting Others

Throughout this book, I have preached that you, as the leader, cannot do it alone. You need the commitment, dedication, and enthusiasm of others. You cannot get this without sharing ownership in the organization and its mission. This principle is equally valid as you set out to develop a vision for the organization. Your people have to share the vision and be excited by and committed to it. At the same time, people look to you for leadership and direction. You obtained your position because of your experience and expertise. You should be as capable as anyone to evaluate what is going on inside and outside the organization and to conceptualize where the organization needs to go. But, don't formulate a vision alone. Two heads are better than one, and for others to be committed, they need to have a say.

A partnership will develop as you ask others what they think is wrong, what they would like to change, and what it is they wish to accomplish. As you share your ideas and seek feedback from your followers, you build an alliance, so that when you get around to articulating a vision, it will be a commonly shared one that your people feel they have had a say in formulating. Your job is to spearhead the development of the vision; then be its champion, enlisting others to join the cause.

Above all else, visions must be inspiring; they must induce others to act in extraordinary ways, to do things better, to improve operations, and to pursue excellence. That requires intensity. Fortunately, intensity is contagious. To the extent that you can remain excited, dedicated, and sincere about a vision, others will join in. Leaders focused upon a vision, like children at play, draw others in.[14]

Leaders bring a vision alive by constantly reminding others of its importance. They preach it, using every opportunity to reinforce the image. They also recognize the importance of their own behavior in symbolizing the aspiration. On the negative side, failure to sustain a "can do" attitude may whittle away faith and commitment of others to the vision. "If the leader doesn't believe we can accomplish the goal, then we must not be able to." On the positive side, leaders can do much to affirm a vision.

In the Federal Bureau of Prisons, one of the most important values is that security is every staff member's responsibility. The vision is for everyone within a facility to be constantly vigilant and committed to maintaining a high degree of security. Margaret Hambrick, former Federal Prisons warden and Regional Director for the Mid-Atlantic Region, tells a story of how one warden affirmed this ethic:

> In one institution, the word spread like wildfire—the warden had written a "shot"—a report on an incident involving a rule violation by an inmate. Not only one, but two! And busted contraband on the food cart going to a housing unit! Writing a shot was not something executives usually did. It certainly made the point—security was everybody's business.[15]

Employees monitor leaders' behaviors; they look for cues about what is important and how to act. Through positive and enthusiastic actions and language, leaders communicate the vision and reassert its importance.

11

STRATEGIC PLANNING

*The art of progress is to preserve order amid
change, and change amid order.*[1]
-- Alfred North Whitehead

In the previous chapter, I argued that prisons need to establish
a vision, that is, an ideal and unique image for their future. They
need to know what it is that they aspire to, what a well-run prison
looks like, and what fundamental values must be assured. But,
visions will remain images of what could be until someone takes
action to realize them. Strategic planning is a process by which
visions can be translated into practice.

The process of developing a vision requires consideration of
what the organization wishes to be. It serves as a fundamental
starting point, but strategic planning moves the process along to
consider three additional issues:

1. How to get there.
2. What actions to take.
3. How to stay on track.[2]

As such, strategic planning incorporates comprehensiveness,
prescription, and control into the process of moving the
organization forward. The act of strategic planning has been
defined as "a disciplined effort to produce fundamental decisions
and actions that shape and guide what an *organization* is, what it
does, and why it does it."[3]

Whereas visioning tends to be an abstract process, strategic
planning is a concrete, orderly, and systematic activity that

involves rational thinking, documentation, control, and monitoring. It focuses attention on how to get from here to there — on objectives and accomplishments. However, its strength may become its weakness in that the high degree of control associated with strategic planning may draw attention away from the mission and serve as a barrier to creativity and innovation.

For example, the staff of a facility may recognize protection of the public as one of their fundamental mandates. In developing a vision of how that mandate becomes manifest, they picture no breaches in the security of the external perimeter, allowing absolutely no chance of an escape. However, an evaluation of current provisions for perimeter security reveals that officers in the towers are the weak link in the system; they are occasionally cited for not maintaining adequate surveillance, they seem to lack enthusiasm, and some are simply biding their time until retirement.

In developing a strategic plan, the facility and its officials may recognize improving correctional practice among wall officers as an objective. The goals may include enhancement of training, more frequent rotation for tower officers, and the initiation of additional monitoring of tower officers, particularly during the late evening and early morning hours. In developing a vision of what should be, studying the issue, and developing goals and a strategy for change, the process is working as it should. However, by setting a procedure into place to "fix" the problem of tower responsibility for perimeter security, the facility runs the risks of failing to consider alternative and more innovative approaches. With a strategic plan in place, administrators can move on to the next problem. Without revisiting the issue, the facility would miss the opportunity to develop a new approach to perimeter security—to tear down the towers and replace human surveillance with electronic surveillance.

Leaders must maintain the balance between strategic action and innovation. Too much attention to what could be results in nothing getting done; too much attention to responding and doing, avoids the ongoing need for thinking about long-term alternatives.

A Seven-Step Strategic Planning Process

There are different models for strategic planning from which an institution or prison system may choose. However, I particularly like the one described by John M. Bryson in his book, *Strategic Planning for Public and Nonprofit Organizations*. The process is well thought out, clearly and simply described in the book, and designed specifically for organizations that do not operate with a profit motive. Bryson lays out a seven-stage process to construct a strategic plan.[4]

1. Introduce strategic planning within the agency

Obviously, the first step in initiating strategic planning begins with someone suggesting the process and the organization making a commitment to it. Within prisons, the initiative is often proposed by the warden or some member of the executive team. In some cases, the directive comes from the central office and strategic planning is introduced throughout the system.

Once a commitment is made, the concept must be introduced throughout the organization. People need to understand its purpose and advantages, how the process works, and what their role will be in its operationalization. This introduction probably begins with an announcement by the chief executive, followed by departmental meetings during which a member of the executive team discusses the concept, and finally succeeded by a series of inservice training workshops.

While the concept is being introduced throughout the organization, the executive team needs to make a few crucial operationalization decisions. This activity involves planning to plan. They need to decide who will be involved in the process. At some level, all members of the organization should have the opportunity to have input, but some members of the organization will be more involved than others. Often, a committee is designated to oversee the process. Ideally, representatives from throughout the organization should be included—members of the executive staff, department heads, and line staff; representatives from all functional areas; and union officials. Executive staff members should be mindful of their influence on people in public meetings. Department heads and line staff are often reluctant to come forward, criticize operations, and propose alternatives. Opportunities for people at different levels within the organization to talk freely should be planned into the process.

Next comes mapping out a schedule. Typically, strategic planning operates on a one-year cycle that coincides in some manner with the budget cycle. The schedule should list each planning activity to be completed and specify when the activity should be finished.

Finally, decisions about getting started have to be made. Many organizations begin with a retreat for the strategic planning committee. At that time, the committee examines steps 2-6 of the planning process. They go back to their respective units, discuss and modify the elements, and then reconvene at some later date to outline the strategic plan.

An important aspect for the executive staff in planning-to-plan is to provide adequate support for the activity. That includes allocating time and resources to allow staff to attend to the process. Executives also have to commit and apportion a significant amount of their own time to be devoted to the activity.

Another important consideration involves building a monitoring and feedback procedure to support the strategic planning process. After devoting a significant amount of time to conceptualizing and writing a plan—activities which take time away from attending to everyday operational issues—it is easy for administrators to slip the plan onto the corner of their desks and return to the business of running the facility. If this happens, strategic planning has not been integrated into the management system as a way of governing facility operations. Monitoring, control, and feedback mechanisms must be in place to oversee and regulate movement toward the goals. Goals need to be revisited and discussed regularly in executive and staff meetings.

Finally, the executive staff needs to plan to celebrate accomplishments. Often, planning gets so routinized that organizations identify goals, develop strategies to accomplish them, carry out those strategies, and then just begin the entire process all over again the next year. They never pause to celebrate their achievements. It is important publicly to review progress and to celebrate. Reinforce what is important by recognizing excellence.

2. Clarify agency mandates

After deciding to incorporate strategic planning into the management of the institution, selecting a strategic planning model, and laying out the procedures, the institution is actually ready to begin planning. This step involves revisiting organizational mandates, that is, the directives imposed upon the institution. For prisons, some mandates are set in law by the legislature; others are defined by directives from the executive branch of government and the supervising agency; and still others are imposed directly or indirectly by judicial decisions about the operations of prisons and the conditions of confinement.

These directives need to be reviewed as they set the parameters in which planning must occur. It is essential to recognize what must be done, what cannot be done, and what is left to discretion. It is also important to attain an understanding of the mandates throughout the organization. One division may understand its own limitations but not those of another functional unit. Broader knowledge of all mandates will facilitate intraorganizational understanding and cooperation.

3. Specify the agency mission and values

Mission statements are succinct declarations of why organizations exist. Typically, they are short, about a paragraph in length, although they can be as short as a lively phrase which captures the spirit of the organization. Clarifying the mission of an institution provides members with a sense of purpose. It defines for them why the organization should be doing what it is doing. As such, the mission is integrally linked to vision, as vision portrays what the organization should look like as it accomplishes its mission.

Bryson suggests that six questions should be considered in formulating a mission statement:

1. What is the organization's identity?
2. What social and political needs does the organization fulfill?
3. What does the organization do to respond to these needs?
4. How does the organization respond to our key stakeholders (anyone affected by or who can affect the operations of the institution)?

5. What are the organization's philosophy and fundamental values?
6. What makes the organization distinctive?[5]

The mission of the federal prison system provides an excellent example of a clear statement that incorporates these six questions:

> The Federal Bureau of Prisons protects society by confining offenders in the controlled environments of prisons and community-based facilities that are safe, humane, and appropriately secure, and which provide work and other self-improvement opportunities to assist offenders in becoming law-abiding citizens.[6]

In answer to the question, "Who are we?", the Federal Bureau of Prisons recognizes that it is a collection of prisons and community-based facilities. These institutions serve the basic social and political need of protecting the public by providing controlled environments for confining offenders. The Bureau responds to this need by assuring that facilities are safe, humane, and appropriately secure and by providing opportunities for self-improvement for offenders. The Bureau's key stakeholders, as outlined by the statement, are society and the confined offenders.

In addition to its mission statement, the Bureau of Prisons has outlined a set of values that it considers central to its identity and mission. These "cultural anchors/core values" are listed on the following page. In reading over the list, it is clear what is important to the federal prison system and how the Bureau is distinctive among prison systems. What's important? The metaphor of family is used to illustrate a close and caring relationship among staff. Staff are expected to perform their duties with integrity and to meet high standards of achievement. The Bureau outlines a unique approach for handling inmates in specifying that the least restrictive measures will be used, all staff are responsible for security, and the dignity of human beings is to be preserved.

The mission and values provide a basis for all planning considerations. Each goal and strategy must be judged against

Cultural Anchors/Core Values

Bureau family

■ The Bureau of Prisons recognizes that staff are the most valuable resource in accomplishing its mission, and is committed to the personal welfare and professional development of each employee. A concept of "Family" is encouraged through healthy, supportive relationships among staff and organization responsiveness to staff needs. The active participation of staff at all levels is essential to the development and accomplishment of organizational objectives.

■ *Sound correctional management*

The Bureau of Prisons maintains effective security and control of its institutions utilizing the least restrictive means necessary, thus proving the essential foundation for sound correctional management programs.

■ *Correctional workers first*

All Bureau of Prisons staff share a common role as correctional workers, which requires a mutual responsibility for maintaining safe and secure institutions and for modeling society's mainstream values and norms.

■ *Promotes integrity*

The Bureau of Prisons firmly adheres to a set of values that promotes honesty and integrity in the professional efforts of its staff to ensure public confidence in the Bureau's prudent use of its allocated resources.

■ *Recognizes the dignity of all*

Recognizing the inherent dignity of all human beings and their potential for change, the Bureau of Prisons treats inmates fairly and responsively and affords them opportunities for self-improvement to facilitate their successful re-entry into the community. The Bureau further recognizes that offenders are incarcerated as punishment, not for punishment.

■ *Career service orientation*

The Bureau of Prisons is a career-oriented service, which has enjoyed a consistent management philosophy and a continuity of leadership, enabling it to evolve as a stable, professional leader in the field of corrections.

■ *Community relations*

The Bureau of Prisons recognizes and facilitates the integral role of the community in effectuating the Bureau's mission, and works cooperatively with other law enforcement agencies, the courts, and other components of government.

■ *High standards*

The Bureau of Prisons requires high standards of safety, security, sanitation, and discipline, which promote a physically and emotionally sound environment for both staff and inmates.[7]

them to determine if they are consistent and will serve to promote the mission. The Bureau of Prisons' selection of the word "anchors" is fitting for the purpose mission serves.

4.   Examine external conditions—threats and opportunities

Once the organization has a foundation to build upon, then it is ready to begin the analytical phase of planning. Steps 4 and 5 consist of an assessment of the conditions influencing the organization both externally and internally. Externally, the organization needs to examine the environmental conditions affecting it, that is, its opportunities and its threats. A number of factors should be examined.

Current social and political trends should be considered. For example, after more than a decade of support for prison expansion, Governor Mario Cuomo stated in a speech that incarceration was not curbing drug offenses and that a shift toward rehabilitation of drug offenders was necessary.[8] It was important for the Department of Correctional Services in New York state to consider the implications of the Governor's comments on its operations. To an extent, the Governor's suggestion could imply a threat to the Department, in that a shift in philosophy could lead to a reduction in prison population and a down-scaling of staff and resources. Alternatively, his comments could denote an opportunity, a chance for the Department to develop new programs and to request additional funding.

Fiscal trends must also be surveyed. Even if the institution believes that a cut in staff would adversely impact its ability to maintain security, declining state revenues may produce reductions. By anticipating the possibility of cuts, the institution may develop a strategy to counter the threat to its resources. Alternatively, a contingency plan can be developed in case the cuts occur.

One of the most rapidly changing areas of prison administration is legal compliance. Mandates are constantly being added and modified in ways that significantly alter prison operations.

Events occurring outside the organization may impact its future. Changes in the workforce may alter who is available to take entry level jobs. A new, lower security facility might open nearby, and senior staff may apply for transfers, leaving the institution with a predominantly rookie staff.

In the course of planning, it is tempting to focus solely on the external threats and ignore the opportunities. The events and situations that place the organization in some kind of risk are the quickest to grab an administrator's attention. But, the organization must also look for opportunities—support for change, new resources, and growth possibilities. Examining external events allows the organization to anticipate changes and to respond effectively before a crisis arises and to capitalize on opportunities.

5. Examine the internal situation—strengths and weaknesses

Just as it is important to consider what is taking place in the world surrounding the institution, it is equally crucial to assess the internal situation, i.e., the facility's weaknesses and strengths. That requires the organization and its people to ask the questions, "what do we do well?" and "what are we struggling with?" To answer these questions, the organization must have performance information.

In the prison business, several performance indicators come to mind—number of escapes, attacks on staff, attacks on inmates, and rule infractions. For these security-related measures to have meaning, they must be compared to something—comparable institutions or trends over time.

Other measures of performance within a prison are also worth monitoring. Staff professionalism is one, the quality of communications is another. Assessing staff and inmate morale provides some indication of how things are going. Analysis of these elements will provide information about which units and disciplines are performing well and which ones may be experiencing problems.

6. Evaluate strategic issues facing the agency

The strategic planning process culminates with the last two steps. In stage 6, based upon the information generated in steps 2 through 5, the organization identifies its strategic issues. In selecting these concerns, the organization makes fundamental policy decisions about how it will proceed in the coming months.

This process is the tough part of the planning because not everyone will agree. Different factions will have different priorities; consequently, conflicts will inevitably arise—about "what will be done (ends), why it will be done (philosophy), how it will be done (means), when it will be done (timing), where it will be done (location), who will do it (group or persons), and who will be advantaged or disadvantaged by it."[9]

The goal of this phase of strategic planning is to construct a list of issues. This task is not as easy as it may seem. Prison executives tend to be problem solvers, and because of this orientation, they want to rush into coming up with the answers, and bypass the issues. But if the organization does not first identify the issues, make sure that they are the actual issues of significant concern which have substantial costs for the institution, and prioritize them, then the organization risks dashing this way and that, from one crisis to the next, without tackling things in a coherent and systematic fashion. By identifying issues, clarifying them, eliminating those that are less pressing, adding ones that have been overlooked, and then proceeding to action, the organization is more likely to make the best use of its resources and time.

The other problem regarding the identification of strategic issues among prison administrators is the tendency to be too "concrete and steel" oriented. A lot of what has to be done around prisons involves the physical plant—sidewalks and plumbing need repair, new buildings need to be added, etc. Administrators, particularly those who do not fully buy into strategic planning, may simply document those projects that must be done during the coming year. For example, one prison devoted a considerable portion of its strategic plan to "upgrading the facilities to meet maintenance needs." Its list of objectives included asbestos removal, shower renovations, replacing a roof, remodeling toilet areas, replacing concertina wire, and installing insulated windows in staff housing. These things would have been done without strategic planning. For this facility, strategic planning served only to document what it had already intended to do. Then why bother?

For strategic planning to guide the facility, the organization must consider its mandate and mission and plan to take actions that will enhance its achievement of those elements. The goals selected by the Federal Correctional Institution at Bastrop, Texas, in 1990 exemplify effective issue identification. Here are three of their 10 goals:

1. Promote inmate personal development and work ethics to eliminate inmate idleness.
2. Develop and monitor sensitivity towards employee personal and professional needs.
3. Promote greater awareness of BOP mission and objectives for dissemination among community and family members.

Each of these issues harkens back to the basic mission and core values of the Bureau of Prisons. If they are accomplished, the Federal Correctional Institution at Bastrop will be a better facility.

The job for leaders in this process is to keep attention focused on issues and to resolve conflicts that arise. The best strategy is to facilitate communication. Various factions need a chance to voice their positions and to hear those of others. Leaders need to promote compromise and to prevent conflict from becoming destructive.

7. Design strategies to respond to issues

The final step in strategic planning is to devise ways to respond to the issues. In the beginning, it is good to be as imaginative as possible; brainstorming is helpful. This allows the institution and the strategic planning team to be creative, to think of new ways of approaching old issues. However, the process needs to quickly move to what is practical. Soon after getting all the alternatives on the table, the strategies should be tested to see if they are feasible. Consider what resources are needed and what must be done to carry out each alternative.

Consider the five strategies identified by the Federal Correctional Institution at Bastrop to accomplish the strategic goal of "developing and monitoring sensitivity towards employee personal and professional needs":

1. Enhance job satisfaction by implementing an individu-alized health and physical fitness program.
2. Establish individual career development plans for all employees.
3. Enhance awareness of career opportunities.
4. Provide Executive Staff support for the mentoring program.
5. Monitor staff morale.

These strategies are reasonable and practical, yet they will move the facility toward accomplishment of its goal. They serve to bridge the gap between existing practices and the core value of "career service."

Getting Started

Experience has shown that strategic planning can assist institutions and prison systems in fulfilling their missions and providing higher quality services; however, implementing strategic planning within the organization is not without difficulties. Without strong commitment to the process by those involved, strategic planning will not be strategic at all but, as I mentioned before, simply an exercise in documenting what would have been done anyway. The benefits of the activity must be widely recognized within the organization and those who will be most directly involved need to be trained. Bryson has made several suggestions about getting started:

1. An organization must be motivated to begin strategic planning. In some instances, that motivation may come from a significant threat. For example, action in federal court may compel the facility to change its conditions of confinement. The facility has no choice other than to change its operations. The facility might also find itself at a turning point, facing a mission change, for example. In other cases, the motivation to plan may

simply flow from the desire to do things better. In any case, the reasons for beginning must be compelling.

2. Next, the program must be advanced, endorsed, and supported by the executive team; otherwise, it will flounder. Key decision-makers define what is important for the organization and its members; their support for strategic planning will signal all staff as to the importance of the activity.

3. Besides having the endorsement of the executive staff, strategic planning must also have a sponsor, someone who will marshal the process along. This individual's role is to maintain enthusiasm within the organization for strategic planning as well as to assure that tasks are completed on schedule. The sponsor must monitor progress, keep all the groups involved, follow through, and keep the process alive. At times, the sponsor will need to facilitate communication between groups. Some groups will need to be encouraged to think more broadly and toward the future rather than documenting what they are already doing.

4. Whatever strategic planning process the organization selects will most likely need to be adapted to the specific situation of the organization. This has to be one of the first decisions. Who is to be involved and how the facility will proceed must be decided in advance.

5. One of the primary tasks of the men and women who manage prisons is to make decisions and solve problems. Because of the nature of prison work, decision-making and problem solving is often reactive. Administrators respond to crises. The purpose behind strategic planning is to be proactive, to establish a basic course for the organization and thereby guide decision-making so that it is consistent with the chosen direction. Key decision-makers must be clear that strategic planning requires them to articulate and discuss what is truly important for the organization. They must then prioritize those issues and set a course to respond to them. This requires the physical presence and participation from those decision-makers!

6. Strategic planning does not require substantial resources, other than the time of organization members. And, there must be a significant commitment of time and attention by those who will be most involved in the process. It takes time to assess the current

situation and reflect on the future, and it requires considerable discussion. Bryson estimates that strategic planning may take up to 10 percent of the work time of key decision-makers. There must be a clear commitment that the benefits of strategic planning justify that level of activity.[10]

Concluding Remarks

Throughout this book, I have frequently remarked that prison work is difficult—it is often trying, usually tense, occasionally dangerous, and almost always frustrating. But, I have also argued that people like to be challenged—they like to do things well and to do useful things. The acts of formulating a vision of success, a mission, and a plan to improve service may serve both to advance the organization toward a set of goals and to help rally staff around a common cause and establish solidarity among them. It may help define for them how their facility is unique and thus provide them with a sense of professional identity.

Leaders should be conscious of these secondary benefits and should use these opportunities to improve staff relations. They can build enthusiasm and commitment as well as give staff a chance to have input into the future direction of the facility. As goals are accomplished and the quality of service improved, leaders can reward and recognize the efforts of staff. The processes associated with looking into the future can thus serve to build team spirit and heighten morale.

12

LEADING INTO THE 21st CENTURY

Specialty training without management development creates situations seen too often in large organizations—in which there are plenty of supervisors and managers, but no real leaders.[1]
-- David W. Helman, Warden, Federal Bureau of Prisons

During the two decade period from 1975 to 1994, prisons experienced unprecedented growth. Inmate populations increased by as much as four times, creating a continuous need for expansion and growth within the system. New prisons have been opened throughout the nation. With this expansion has come a steady increase in staff positions with an accompanying demand for mid- and upper-level managers in correctional organizations.

Increased opportunities for upward mobility have been good for morale. The time until promotion has been greatly compressed, and this, along with the chance for added responsibility and more pay, has helped sustain vitality and enthusiasm. This situation has in some ways been analogous to that of the military during times of war—the risks are greater than in peace time, but soldiers have the occasion to do what they are trained to do. The challenges and demands are increased, and these factors tend to have positive influences on morale. Furthermore, war provides for accelerated promotions; this too has a positive influence. Rapid expansion of prisons and their populations has created stress for prison employees and officials, but also has provided significant personal opportunities for advancement and accomplishment.

The situation within prison service is about to change. Projections indicate that this period of growth in incarceration will reach its peak in the mid-1990s and will remain flat, if not decline, in the coming years. Furthermore, government fiscal crises and fiscal conservativism will result in lower budgets for prison systems with correspondingly fewer funds for new programs, equipment, and salaries. Since the period of expansion has been going on for approximately 20 years, and most states and the federal system have either 20- or 25-year retirement programs, the experience of most employees working in prisons is limited to this exceptional period of growth and opportunity. For many staff, the coming period of decline may feel particularly painful, unfair, and even punitive.

So prison executives face a new challenge. While moving into a time with fewer opportunities, they must keep hope alive among their people. They must maintain vitality, enthusiasm, and motivation within their organizations. John Gardner suggests that leaders conceive of a future for the organization that will inspire their people to overcome adversity and work together toward higher ends.[2] That is exactly the challenge for prison executives facing the 21st century; they must stimulate their people to maintain high standards of service in the face of dwindling resources and apparent declining support from state or federal governments.

The Leadership Challenge

Every prison executive I have ever met seems to recognize that the sidewalks around the compound deteriorate over time; concrete breaks and crumbles as it is affected by weather and wear. Consequently, sidewalks must be attended to constantly; they can be repaired in some cases, but sometimes they must be torn out and rebuilt.

I'm not equally convinced that all prison executives recognize that the social fabric of their organizations also crumbles over time. Motivation declines and values disintegrate. Structures and processes that were appropriate during a particular phase of the institution's life are no longer suitable for an entirely new set of problems.[3] But, organizations—as entities composed of human beings—tend to mature much like individuals. As they age, they get set in their ways. Customary ways of doing things—written and unwritten procedures and standardization—lock institutions into routines that can become outdated and inappropriate, block needed innovations, and grind efficiency to a halt.

To attend to the organizational "sidewalks" of an institution, John Gardner suggests that leaders must promote a continual process of *renewal*; an activity that "encompasses both continuity and change, reinterpreting tradition to meet new conditions, building a better future on an acknowledged heritage."[4] If prisons are entering a period of diminishing resources and opportunities, surely the tendency will be for employees to feel the effects, to be more likely to become disgruntled, dissatisfied, and alienated, and to feel unappreciated and frustrated. Leaders must counter this trend by helping their people find meaning and fulfillment within prison work and the changing environment in which they work.

Sounds good. But how do you do it? In the face of adversity, how do you reenergize people? How do you keep them from becoming estranged or slipping into complacency? How do you maintain their commitment to a set of fundamental values about prison service and quality conditions of confinement?

A common tendency during hard times is to hunker down, to circle the wagons, and to fight for traditions. But, as Gardner so aptly points out, you must accommodate both continuity and change,[5] which involves opening up and taking some risks. You must create a climate in which people feel safe enough to let you know what's wrong and what they think should be done about it. You have to be willing to make mistakes and to allow others to make mistakes; otherwise, innovation is not possible.

Here are some actions Gardner suggests to promote renewal:

1. Release the talent and energy of your people

In a crisis, managers usually want to maintain control and, therefore, tend to draw decision-making back toward themselves. During a situation such as that currently developing in prison administration, where diminishing resources and opportunities is going to engender a crisis at some level while simultaneously leaving staff feeling dissatisfied, further removal of staff from decision-making will probably heighten their dissatisfaction. This, in turn, will push the institution further into crisis, and the potential for amplifying the problem will build.

So, if you have a crisis on your hands (and I am not referring to an inmate disturbance where centralized control is absolutely necessary, but rather an administrative crisis), it seems that you would want to seek out individuals with new ideas, imagination, and originality. If the old ways are failing the system, then new ideas need to be invented; that requires fresh thinking. Who might be better positioned to come up with innovative ideas than your own personnel? Bring them into the decision-making loop. Share information about what is happening and get their feedback and ideas. And, most importantly, give them responsibility.

2. Rotate personnel

If correctional officers stay in correctional services and remain responsible for institutional security, and treatment personnel stay in the treatment division and remain responsible for release preparation, and administrative personnel stay in administrative services and remain responsible for fiscal and bureaucratic duties, and the three functions fail to communicate effectively or appreciate the activities of the other two functions, and periodically a new chief executive is promoted out of one of the three divisions who does not really understand either of the other two functions, then... you have problem! So what's the solution? A well-planned program of personnel rotation will not only result in individual renewal by providing new challenges and opportunities, but will also produce significant organizational benefits. Reassignment across disciplines promotes understanding of all aspects of institutional management; it tends to reduce hostility and to increase communication. Rotation also helps prepare generalists for eventual assumption of the highest posts within the organization.

3. Motivate

When morale is spiraling downward, what do you need? You need your most inspirational speakers, your best coaches, your preachers. You need a revival, an event that will reaffirm the fundamental principles that undergird the institution and will awaken the spirit within individuals.

As you begin to think about renewal, make two lists of the most influential people in your organization. One list should identify those individuals who best inspire people; the other should list your most cynical yet influential personnel. Some individuals will be influential (positively or negatively) because of their formal position within the organization; others will be influential because of their personalities. Once the lists are made, a strategy must be designed to develop a constituency for renewal using the positive influence of one group and a counter plan to negate the influence of the other group. Meet with those individuals who are most likely to be good motivators and try to enlist their support.

4. Make sure you haven't replaced the ends with the means

The purpose of rules and procedures is to create order and orderliness within an organization, and nowhere is that more important than in running prisons. As I have pointed out before, men and women attracted to prison service tend to be comfortable with its uniformity, regularity, and control. But rules, procedures, and customary ways of doing things are a means to an end, a way to achieve safe, humane, and productive prisons. They must not become ends in themselves, so that you and others within the organization are working solely to preserve them. You must reevaluate their usefulness. No better way exists than to ask staff who have to abide by them. Reality checks come from first-hand contacts.

5. Open up communication

When they pull in the wagons, senior level administrators risk cutting themselves off from communication with those below them in the organization and those outside the organization. They hear less, and end up rather stubbornly clinging to convictions that served them well in the past, causing them to miss alternative solutions to current situations.[6]

So, talk and listen! Solicit advice from throughout the facility. And, be careful to avoid falling into the committee trap, where a committee exists for everything, and there is lots of conversation, but little innovation. Committees can serve as useful structures to facilitate group discussions and group decision-making, but can also become bureaucratic impediments when they become weighted down by custom, routine, and the status quo, thereby inhibiting any consideration of new approaches.

Importantly, leaders must seek information from outside. Insiders have vested interests and loyalties that shade their judgments. Outsiders can be honest. They may have perspectives that are unavailable within the organization.

If you want to be a leader as prison service moves toward the 21st century, if you want to be a hero, if you want to serve your facility and its people, then you must heed the trends that are evolving and attend, now more than ever, to organizational *renewal*. You must prepare your organization for a different time— a more difficult situation—and you must sustain and support your people and the facility as they react to the changing environment.

As any organization moves from one developmental stage to another, new leadership is needed. I illustrated this principle earlier with the example of how Norman Carlson recommended J. Michael Quinlan to succeed him as director when the Federal Bureau of Prisons entered a different era. Perhaps, the greatest legacy you can leave your institution is to develop the next generation of leaders. This one responsibility may offer you the best prospect for renewing your organization. But remember, renewal will be possible only if you do not recreate yourself in the next generation of leaders.

Leadership Development

Being a prison warden is a demanding position with diverse responsibilities. Let's pause for a moment and consider what wardens need to know:

1. They must be well versed in prison security and able to devise systems to protect the public, staff, and inmates.

2. Wardens need to know something about managing people.

3. They must have a working knowledge of food service.

4. They must have a grasp of maintenance of the physical plant and its grounds. They need to be sufficiently informed to decide whether the boiler really needs to be replaced and if the back-up generator is adequate.

5. They have to be public relations oriented and able to effectively interact with the community and media.

6. They must read and understand financial statements, prepare budgets, and oversee the fiscal operations of a multimillion dollar facility.

7. They must know something about education—basic, secondary, literacy training, occupational training, and higher education.

8. They must be sufficiently informed to speak intelligently with psychologists, shop foremen, and coaches because wardens will have to make decisions regarding all disciplines.

9. They must be aware of occupational safety and health and environmental protection regulations.

10. They must be familiar with basic rules of law and well versed in legal compliance.

11. They must have an understanding of personnel policy.

12. They must be able to plan.

Let's quit there. Obviously, the job is enormous and one which requires knowledge and expertise in many areas. As an educator, I am overwhelmed by the list because there is no way that I can provide young people with all the information they need to know to be effective prison wardens. It is simply too much information.

Some say that prison workers and potential wardens do not need college degrees, that they will learn all they need to know on the job. I think not. Clearly, a college education will not and cannot provide individuals with sufficient information needed to be wardens (particularly since what students learn today may not be relevant five years from now). What an education does, however, is equip individuals with the skills to more effectively learn to be prison wardens. A college education should make individuals better consumers of information, and it should increase the students' ability to assimilate, analyze, synthesize, and use information for decision-making. Higher education should produce more critical thinkers. It should broaden peoples' perspectives and deepen their understanding. A college education should increase the students' understanding of human behavior, acquaint them with the interactions and processes of groups, provide them with some sense of history, and open their minds to the influence of culture. It does not matter what degree potential wardens receive, and a criminal justice or criminology degree is certainly not necessary. Because warden jobs are so diverse, they require individuals who are good learners. Students with broad educational foundations will be most successful in acquiring the information necessary to be wardens.

Strong educational preparation is just the first step in the making of a good warden. Personnel selection processes tend to look for excellence in trying to identify future executives, so when a young staff member who is a particularly good correctional officer or an excellent caseworker is observed, we begin to consider that person for promotion and keep our eye on him or her. But, just because someone is a good correctional officer does not mean that the person will make a good manager; one set of skills does not necessarily translate into the other. All of us have seen the Peter Principle in action when good workers rise to their level of incompetence.

Organizations can help avoid the Peter Principle by recognizing that people need to be prepared to assume leadership positions. Some individuals have natural talents that assist them as leaders; they are effective communicators, charismatic, and dynamic. They have the capacity to motivate and the self-confidence to make strategic decisions. They inspire trust and diligence. Selection, therefore, plays a role in the maintenance of a pool of effective leaders. Still, men and women with leadership talent do not necessarily live up to their potential, and individuals with fewer natural talents can develop into highly effective leaders.

Some leadership characteristics—intelligence, vitality, confidence, charisma, and courage—cannot be greatly influenced since they are closely tied to personality and develop across an entire span of life. But other desirable qualities can be taught: understanding followers, ability to deal with people, motivational skills, and decision-making. To this list, the Federal Bureau of Prisons adds in its Leadership Forum (a program to prepare mid-level managers to assume top level positions) these: public policy analysis, legal issues, ethics, media relations, cultural diversity, labor-management relations, employee recruitment and retention, and affirmative action.

The total development of a leader with these skills cannot be achieved in a short, one-shot effort but instead requires a multifaceted approach. Short, single-topic in-service training sessions are helpful. One warden that I know runs his own small program. He selects 10-12 employees from all ranks and disciplines and offers several, week-long symposiums in which different leadership topics are covered each week.

Longer, higher-visibility programs also have a role in leadership development. The Federal Bureau of Prisons runs its Leadership Forum several times each year. High-potential, mid-level managers are brought to Washington, D.C., for a week of training. This program not only provides participants with needed information but also is a great motivator. By singling out these individuals and giving them special treatment, the Forum bolsters their willingness and confidence to assume leadership positions.

Perhaps, the single most important phase of leadership development is the chance to try things and to receive feedback. Helping professions, psychology and social work, have recognized the worth of this process and have formalized it—they call it, "supervision." Therapists met with other therapists, usually on a weekly basis, to discuss cases. Leaders need similar opportunities to discuss problems, approaches, and issues, particularly with other more experienced leaders.

When discussed in leadership circles, this process is often referred to as "mentoring." But I think the supervision approach used by therapists is a good model to follow, where mentor and mentoree meet on a weekly basis with a set agenda to discuss how the mentoree is doing as a leader. This approach will not only provide the short-term benefit of helping the individual with current problems, but will also help develop the individual as a leader over the long run.

As individuals move up within an organization, the activities for which they are responsible broaden until they are eventually expected to handle the long and diverse set of activities listed above for wardens. Given this trajectory, it is essential that leaders be rotated through different functional areas. They need to understand a broad spectrum of institutional activities. Furthermore, new assignments keep the best and brightest challenged.

As a leader who is concerned with the facility, its personnel and its future, you have an obligation to develop leaders. Along with all the other demands on your time, you must add leadership development to your plate, not on some *ad hoc*, occasional basis, but as an ongoing and formal task. You need to be constantly observing young staff for leadership potential, and be sure you do not suppress their potential. Keep them out of alienating circumstances and provide them with challenges. You must scan the horizon and ask yourself where things are going (i.e., what external threats and opportunities are developing) and what type of leaders will be needed to meet coming demands.

People with Commitment

Emile Durkheim, noted French sociologist, coined the term, *anomie*, to describe a state marked by the absence of norms or values. Durkheim and sociologists who followed have demonstrated that during times of adversity, social commitment to norms and values dissolve and a state of anomie results. During a time of anomie, commitment tends to disintegrate since it becomes ambiguous as to what one should be committed to.

If, as I have suggested, prisons are entering a period in which growth ceases and corresponding reductions in opportunities occur, then commitment among prison employees may be at stake. If chances for promotion and salary increases decline, occasions to start new programs become limited, and supplies become more restricted, prison employees may question the support and care offered by prison employment. Consequently, a major challenge for prison leaders in the coming decade will be maintenance of commitment to high performance and quality incarceration.

This idea of commitment is tricky, particularly during crises. Mindless allegiance to the organization and accepted practices will assure its eventual failure. On one hand, commitment gives meaning to institutional endeavors. It serves as the rallying point around which pride and loyalty develop. What people are committed to within the organization helps them define their own professional identities, and allows them to collectively formulate an institutional identity; however, an uncritical allegiance will result in failure to adapt to new conditions. Organizations must undergo a constant and continuous process of reinterpreting commitment to meet changing present and future conditions.

As a contemporary prison leader, you face the extraordinary challenge of inspiring your people to look beyond their current losses of opportunities and uniting them toward finding effective ways of achieving self-fulfillment and maintaining high-quality incarceration. You must help your people make commitments beyond themselves; assist them in achieving self-respect by protecting the public and serving prisoners well; give them a say in things so they will have ownership in the decision-making processes of the institution; and develop their loyalty by assuring that their affiliation with the institution gives personal meaning and pride to their lives. You must keep *hope* alive!

NOTES

Chapter 1
GOVERNING PRISONS

1. Bert Useem, "How Do We Govern Our 'Cities'?" *Corrections Today* 52 (February, 1990): 88-94.

2. Bert Useem and Peter Kimball, *States of Siege: U.S. Prison Riots 1971-1986* (New York: Oxford University Press, 1989).

3. John J. DiIulio, Jr., *Governing Prisons: A Comparative Study of Correctional Management* (New York: Free Press, 1987).

4. Ibid., p. 242.

5. Useem and Kimball, *States of Siege*, pp. 218-219.

6. DiIulio, *Governering Prisons*, p. 242.

7. Donald R. Cressey, *The Prison: Studies in Institutional Organization and Change* (New York: Holt, Rinehart and Winston, 1961), p. 11.

8. David Duffee, *Correctional Management: Change & Control in Correctional Organizations* (Prospect Heights, Illinois: Waveland Press, 1980).

9. Lynne Goodstein and Doris MacKenzie, eds., *The American Prison: Issues in Research and Policy* (New York: Plenum Press, 1989).

10. Todd R. Clear and George F. Cole, *American Corrections*, 2nd ed. (Pacific Grove, California: Brooks/Cole, 1990), p. 151.

11. DiIulio, *Governing Prisons*, pp. 11-12.

12. John J. DiIulio, Jr., "Prisons that Work--Management is the Key," *Federal Prisons Journal* 1 (Summer, 1990): 8.

13. J. Michael Quinlan, "What Should the Public Expect From Prisons--Overcoming the Myths," *Federal Prisons Journal* 1 (Summer, 1990): p. 6.

14. Robert K. Merton, *Social Theory and Social Structure* (New York: Free Press, 1957), p. 200.

15. Harry Cohen, *The Demonics of Bureaucracy* (Ames, Iowa: Iowa State University Press, 1965), p. 15.

16. Alvin W. Cohn, "The Failure of Correctional Management," *Crime and Delinquency* 19 (July, 1973): 329.

17. John W. Gardner, *On Leadership* (New York: Free Press, 1990), p. 1.

18. G. Ronald Gilbert, "Making Government a 'Quality' Place to Work," *Government Executive* (November, 1989): 58.

19. Ibid.

20. DiIulio, *Governing Prisons*, pp. 236-241 argues for bureaucratically organized prisons.

21. Gardner, *On Leadership*, p. 109.

22. Ibid., p. 49.

Part 2
RUNNING A TIGHT (BUT LOOSE) SHIP

1. Thomas J. Peters and Robert H. Waterman, *In Search of Excellence: Lessons from America's Best Run Companies* (New York: Warner Books, 1982), pp. 13-16.

Chapter 2
PAYING ATTENTION TO DETAIL

1. Peters and Waterman, *In Search of Excellence*, p. 13.

2. Quoted in Clear and Cole, *American Corrections*, pp. 69-71.

3. This example was provided to the author by Margie J. Phelps of the Kansas Department of Corrections.

4. Ronald Burkhart, "Essential Elements for Effective Leadership and Management," mimeograph, Federal Correctional Institution, Fort Worth, Texas.

5. DiIulio, *Governing Prisons*.

6. James M. Kouzes and Barry Z. Posner, *The Leadership Challenge: How to Get Extraordinary Things Done in Organizations* (San Francisco: Jossey-Bass, 1988), pp. 16-19.

7. Perry M. Smith, *Taking Charge--Making the Right Decisions* (Garden City Park, New York: Avery Publishing Group, 1988), pp. 93-96.

8. Tom Peters, *Thriving on Chaos: Handbook for a Management Revolution* (New York: Harper & Row, 1987), p. 628.

9. Ibid, p. 12.

Chapter 3
CREATING QUALITY PRISONS

1. Kouzes and Posner, *The Leadership Challenge*, pp. 195-196.

2. Mark S. Fleisher, *Warehousing Violence* (Newbury Park: Sage Publications), 1989.

3. James MacGregor Burns, *Leadership* (New York: Harper Torchbooks, 1978), p.20.

4. Kouzes and Posner, *The Leadership Challenge*, p. 193.

5. Tom Peters and Nancy Austin, *A Passion for Excellence: The Leadership Difference* (New York: Random House, 1985), p. 265.

6. Warren Bennis, *The Unconscious Conspiracy: Why Leaders Can't Lead* (New York: AMACOM, 1976), p. 174.

7. Peters and Austin, *A Passion for Excellence*, p. 270.

8. George Camp, speech given at the Wardens' Conference, Federal Bureau of Prisons, Minnesota, June 20, 1990.

9. Morgan W. McCall, Jr. and Michael M. Lombardo, "What Makes a Top Executive?" *Psychology Today* 17 (February, 1983): 26-31.

10. Robert N. Bellah, Richard Madsen, William M. Sullivan, Ann Swidler, and Steven M. Tipton, *Habits of the Heart: Individualism, and Commitment in American Life* (New York: Harper & Row, 1985), p. 167.

11. Gardner, *On Leadership*, p. 195.

12. George Orwell, *The Road to Wigan Pier* (San Diego: Harcourt Brace Jovanovich, 1958), p. 194.

13. Max DePree, *Leadership Is an Art* (New York: Doubleday, 1989), p. 45.

14. Ibid., pp. 45-53.

Chapter 4
DEVELOPING PEOPLE

1.   DiIulio, *Governing Prisons*, p. 239.

2.   Eric D. Poole and Robert M. Regoli, "Professionalism, Role Conflict, Work Alienation and Anomie: A Look at Prison Management," *The Social Science Journal* 20 (January, 1983): 63-70.

3.   Gardner, *On Leadership*, p. 185.

4.   Edwin P. Hollander and Lynn R. Offermann, "Power and Leadership in Organizations: Relationships in Transition," *American Psychologist* 45 (February, 1990): 179-189; K. I. Miller and P. R. Monge, "Participation, Satisfaction and Productivity: A Meta-Analytic Review," *Academy of Management Journal* 29 (1986): 727-753; and C. R. Leana, "Power Relinguishments versus Powersharing: Theoretical Clarification and Empirical Comparison of Delegation and Participation," *Journal of Applied Psychology* 72 (1987): 228-233.

5.   DePree, *Leadership Is an Art*, p. 10.

6.   Ibid., pp. 10 and 1.

7.   Peter Block, *The Empowered Manager: Positive Political Skills at Work* (San Francisco: Jossey-Bass, 1990), pp.80-81.

8.   F. J. Roethlisberger and William J. Dickson, *Management and the Worker* (Cambridge, MA: Harvard University Press, 1949).

9.   Gardner, *On Leadership*, p. 185.

10. Patricia Renwick and Edward E. Lawler III, "What You Really Want From Your Job," *Psychology Today* 12 (1978): 56.

11. Arnold Tannenbaum, *Control in Organizations* (New York: McGraw Hill, 1968).

12. W. W. Burke, "Leadership as Empowering Others," in *Executive Power: How Executives Influence People and Organizations*, ed. Suresh Srivasta (San Francisco: Jossey-Bass, 1986), pp. 51-77.

13. Hollander and Offermann, "Power and Leadership in Organizations," p. 183.

14. Nancy C. Jurik and Russell Winn, "Describing Correctional-Security Dropouts and Rejects--An Individual and Organizational Profile," *Criminal Justice and Behavior* 14 (1987): 5-25.

15. William G. Saylor and Kevin N. Wright, "A Comparative Study of the Relationship of Status and Longevity in Determining Perceptions of Work Environment Among Federal Employees," *Journal of Offender Rehabilitation* 17 (1992): 133-160.

16. A. Guenther and M. Guenther, "Screws Vs. Thugs," *Society* 12 (1974): 42-50; S. Stalgaitis, A. Meyers, and J. Krisak, "A Social Learning Theory for Reduction of Correctional Officer Stress," *Federal Probation* 3 (1982) 33-41; and J. B. Stinchcomb, "Correctional Officer Stress: Looking at the Causes, You May Be the Cure," paper presented at the annual meetings of the Academy of Criminal Justice Sciences, Orlando, Florida.

17. Kouzes and Posner, *The Leadership Challenge*, p. 174.

18. Peters and Austin, *A Passion for Excellence*, p. 216.

19. Rosabeth M. Kanter, *The Change Masters: Innovation for Productivity in the American Corporation* (New York: Simon & Schuster, 1983).

20. Quoted by Kouzes and Posner, *The Leadership Challenge*, p. 161.

21. Gardner, *On Leadership*, p. 36.

22. Ibid.

23. Ibid., p. 26.

24. Hollander and Offermann, "Power and Leadership in Organizations," p. 184.

25. Tom Peters, "Forward," in *The Leadership Challenge*, Kouzes and Posner, p. xii.

26. Kouzes and Posner, *The Leadership Challenge*, pp. 162-166.

27. Kevin N. Wright, "Prison Leadership: A Strategy for Success in the 1990's." *Federal Prisons Journal* 2 (Summer, 1991): 9-10.

28. P. S. Goodman, R. Devadas, and T. L. Hughson. "Groups and Productivity: Analyzing the Effectiveness of Self-Managing Teams," in *Productivity in Organizations*, eds. J. P. Campbell and R. J. Campbell (San Francisco: Jossey-Bass, 1988), pp. 295-327.

29. Hollander and Offermann, "Power and Leadership in Organizations," p. 184.

30. Doug Lansing, Joseph B. Bogan, and Loren Karacki, "Unit Management: Implementing a Different Correctional Approach," *Federal Probation* 41 (March 1977): 43-49.

31. Ibid.

Chapter 5
CREATING COMMUNITY, BUILDING TEAMWORK, AND ACTING LIKE FAMILY

1. Dean Tjosvold, *Working Together to Get Things Done* (Lexington: D.C. Heath, 1986), p. 25.

2. Thomas J. Watson, Jr., *A Business and Its Beliefs: The Ideas That Helped Build IBM* (New York: McGraw-Hill, 1963), p. 5.

3. Philip Selznick, *Leadership in Administration: A Sociological Interpretation* (New York: Harper & Row, 1957), p. 28.

4. Peters and Waterman, *In Search of Excellence*, p. 285.

5. Eric D. Poole and Robert M. Regoli, "Alienation in Prison-- An Examination of the Work Relations of Prison Guards," *Criminology* 19 (August, 1981): 251-270.

6. Fleisher, *Warehousing Violence*, p. 209.

7. Ibid.

8. David J. Abramis, "All Work and No Play Isn't Even Good for Work," *Psychology Today* 23 (March, 1989): 34-38.

9. Daniel Katz and Robert L. Kahn, *The Social Psychology of Organizations* (New York: John Wiley & Sons, 1966), pp. 370-380.

10. Depree, *Leadership Is an Art*, p. 14.

11. Gardner, *On Leadership*, p. 191.

12. Kouzes and Posner, *The Leadership Challenge*, pp. 114-115.

13. George Lakoff and Mark Johnson, *Metaphors We Live By* (Chicago: University of Chicago Press, 1980), p. 146.

14. Gardner, *On Leadership*, p. 19.

15. Kouzes and Posner, *The Leadership Challenge*, pp. 125-129.

16. Ibid., pp. 168-169.

17. DePree, *Leadership Is an Art*, pp. 9-10.

18. Peters, *Thriving on Chaos*, p. 609.

19. Block, *The Empowered Manager*, pp. 90-91.

20. Peters, *Thriving on Chaos*, pp. 611-612.

21. Carl Rogers, *On Becoming a Person* (Boston: Houghton Mifflin, 1961).

22. J. W. Driscoll, "Trust and Participation in Organizational Decision Making as Predictors of Satisfaction," *Academy of Management Journal* 21 (1978): 44-56.

23. Kouzes and Posner, *The Leadership Challenge*, p. 156.

24. Charles F. Kiefer and Peter Stroh, "A New Paradigm for Developing Organizations," in *Transforming Work*, ed. John D. Adams (Alexandria, Virginia: Miles River Press, 1984).

Chapter 6
PULLING IT TOGETHER

1.   Leo Carroll, *Hacks, Blacks, and Cons* (Lexington, Mass.: D.C. Heath, 1974), p. 52.

2.   Carroll, *Hacks, Blacks, and Cons*; John Irwin, *Prisons in Turmoil* (Boston: Little, Brown, 1980); James Jacobs, *Statesville: The Penitentiary in Mass Society* (Chicago: University of Chicago Press, 1977); Charles Stastny and Gabrielle Tyrnauer, *Who Rules the Joint?* (Lexington, Mass.: Lexington Books, 1982).

3.   Carroll, *Hacks, Blacks and Cons*, p. 52.

4.   Irwin, *Prisons in Turmoil*.

5.   Kathleen Engel and Stanley Rothman, "Prison Violence and the Paradox of Reform." *The Public Interest* 73 (Fall, 1983): 91-105.

6.   James B. Jacobs, *Statesville*, p. 85.

7.   Ben M. Crouch and James W. Marquart, "Resolving the Paradox of Reform: Litigation, Prisoner Violence, and Perceptions of Risk." *Justice Quarterly* 7 (March, 1990): 103-123.

8.   Jacobs, *Statesville*, p. 103.

9.   Ibid., pp. 99, 103-104, and 209-211.

10. Paul T. Hill, Gail E. Foster, and Tamar Gendler, "High Schools with Character: Alternatives to Bureaucracy," (Santa Montica: The RAND Corporation, 1990).

11. Robert D. McFadden, "New York City Study Urges Methods to Improve Schools," *New York Times*, October 22, 1990, p. B3.

12. Where people are held against their will, neither a therapeutic nor a democratic arrangement can be realized. I am not suggesting that inmates cannot be reformed nor that inmates or staff should have no opportunities for self determination, but there must be leaders who take responsibility and initiative for running safe, clean, and productive facilities.

13. Gardner, *On Leadership*, p. 127.

14. Smith, *Taking Charge*, pp. 2-3.

15. Peter Block, *The Empowered Manager*, p. 11.

16. Francis Bacon, *Essays* (New York: Macmillan, 1930).

17. Block, *The Empowered Manager*, p. 65.

Part III
PRISONERS

1. Quinlan, "What Should the Public Expect," p. 6.

2. Robert Johnson, *Hard Time: Understanding and Reforming the Prison* (Monterey, California: Brooks/Cole, 1987), p. 50.

3. John P. Conrad, "Where There's Hope, There's Life," in *Justice as Fairness: Perspectives on the Justice Model*, eds. David Fogel and Joe Hudson (Cincinnati: Anderson, 1981), p. 17.

4. Lyndon Nelmes, "The Front Line," *Corrections Today* 50 (April 1988): 22.

5. Conrad, "Where There's Hope," pp. 18-19. Conrad also includes a seventh right, to vote, which to me poses political implications that falls beyond the scope of this discussion.

Chapter 7
SAFETY, CARE, DIGNITY AND RESPECT

1. Albert K. Cohen, "Prison Violence," in *Prison Violence*, eds. Albert K. Cohen, George F. Cole, and Robert G. Bailey (Lexington: Lexington Books, 1975), p. 19.

2. J. Forbes Farmer, "A Case Study in Regaining Control of a Violent State Prison," *Federal Probation* 52 (March, 1988): 41-52.

3. Olin Minton, "National Institute of Corrections Technical Assistance Report of Massachusetts Department of Corrections," (Washington, DC: National Institute of Corrections, 1979), p. 8.

4. Farmer, "A Case Study in Regaining Control," p. 42-45.

5. Ibid., pp. 44-46.

6. See Kevin N. Wright and Lynne Goodstein, "Correctional Environments," in *The American Prison*, eds. Goodstein and MacKenzie, p. 259 for a discussion of new generation facilities.

7. S.H. Gettinger, *New Generation Jails: An Innovative Approach to an Age-old Problem* (Washington, DC: National Institute of Corrections, 1984); L.L. Zupan, B.A. Menke, and N.P. Lovrich, "Podular/direct Supervision Detention Facilities: Challenges for Human Resource Development," in *Proceedings of the First Annual Symposium on New Generation Jails*, eds. J. Farbstein and R. Wener (Boulder, CO: National Institute of Corrections Jail Center, 1986); and W.R. Nelson, M. O'Toole, B. Krauth, and C.G. Whitmore, *Direct Supervision Models* (Boulder, CO: National Institute of Corrections Information Center, 1984).

8. R. Wener, W. Frazier, and J. Farbstein, "Jails: Direct-Supervision Facilities Have Succeeded in a Field Better Known for Its Failures," *Psychology Today* 21 (June, 1987): pp. 40-47.

9. Hans Toch, "Social Climate and Prison Violence," in *Prison Violence in America*, eds. Michael Braswell, Steven Dillingham, and Reid Montgomery, Jr. (Cincinnati: Anderson, 1985), pp. 41-42.

10. Ibid., p. 43.

11. Fleisher, *Warehousing Violence*, p. 65.

12. Ibid., pp. 64-86.

13. Ibid., pp. 86-87.

14. James W. Marquart, "Prison Guards and the Use of Physical Coercion as a Mechanism of Prisoner Control," *Criminology* 24 (1986): 355.

15. Fleisher, *Warehousing Violence*, p. 174.

16. In Estelle v. Gamble (1976) the court specified that deliberate indifference to an inmate's medical needs violates the Eighth Amendment as it constitutes the unnecessary and wanton infliction of pain.

17. Farmer, "A Case Study in Regaining Control," p. 44.

18. Wright and Goodstein, "Correctional Environments," p. 256.

19. Daniel Glaser, *The Effectiveness of a Prison and Parole System* (New York: Bobbs-Merrill, 1964).

20. Gordon Hawkins, *The Prison: Policy and Practice* (Chicago: University of Chicago Press, 1976), p. 92.

21. John Hepburn, "Prison Guards as Agents of Social Control," in *The American Prison*, eds. Goodstein and MacKenzie, pp. 195-196.

22. Ibid., pp. 194-197.

23. Ibid., p. 197.

24. Fleisher, *Warehousing Violence*, p. 174.

25. Ibid. p. 48.

26. Hawkins, *The Prison*, p. 105.

Chapter 8
A PRODUCTIVE ENVIRONMENT

1. Lyndon Nelmes, "The Front Line," *Corrections Today* 50 (April, 1988): p. 22.

2. Ibid.

3. Norval Morris, *The Future of Imprisonment* (Chicago: University of Chicago Press, 1974).

4. Stephen Schafer, *The Political Criminal--The Problem of Morality and Crime* (New York: Free Press, 1974).

5. Johnson, *Hard Time*, p. 182.

6. Statement made by my wife, Karen, one morning as we discussed the influence we have on the lives of our children.

7. Kevin N. Wright, "Prison Environment and Behavioral Outcomes," *Journal of Offender Rehabilitation* 20 (1993): 93-113.

8. Warren E. Burger, "Factories with Fences," address delivered at the commencement exercises of Pace University on June 11, 1983, New York, New York. Reprinted in Kenneth C. Haas and Geoffrey P. Alpert (eds.) *The Dilemmas of Punishment* (Prospect Heights, Illinois: Waveland Press, 1986), pp. 349-356.

9. Max Grünhut, *Penal Reform: A Comparative Study* (Oxford: Clarendon Press, 1948), p. 198.

10. Hawkins, *The Prison*, pp. 114.

11. Quoted by Hawkins, *The Prison*, p. 115.

12. John Conrad, "What Do the Undeserving Deserve?" in *The Pains of Imprisonment*, eds. Robert Johnson and Hans Toch (Beverly Hills: Sage Publications, 1982), p. 328.

13. Office of Research, "Post Release Employment Project: Summary of Findings," Federal Bureau of Prisons, Washington, D.C., May 22, 1991.

14. Timothy J. Flanagan, "Prison Labor and Industry," in *The American Prison*, eds. Goodstein and MacKenzie, pp. 155-157.

15. Office of Research, "Post Release Employment Project."

16. Flanagan, "Prison Labor and Industry," p. 144.

17. Ibid., 153-154.

18. Robert C. Grieser, "Model Approaches--Examining Prison Industry That Works," *Corrections Today* 50 (August, 1988): 176.

19. Ibid, pp. 176 & 178.

20. Flanagan, "Prison Labor and Industry," pp. 149-150.

21. Hal Farrier, "Secure Prison Industries--Getting the Benefits Without the Risks," *Corrections Today* 51 (July, 1989): 110 and 112.

22. Flanagan, "Prison Labor and Industry," p. 155.

23. Robert Martinson, "What Works? Questions and Answers about Prison Reform." *The Public Interest* 35 (1974): 22-54. See also Douglas C. Lipton, Robert Martinson, and Judith Wilks, *The Effectiveness of Correctional Treatment* (New York: Praeger, 1975).

24. Nelmes, "The Front Line," p. 46.

25. Morris, *The Future of Imprisonment*, p. 14.

26. Ibid. pp. 14-15.

27. Clear and Cole, *American Corrections*, pp. 345-347.

28. Ibid.

29. Ibid., p. 347.

30. Peter Schmidt and Ann D. Witte, *An Economic Analysis of Crime and Justice: Theory, Methods, and Applications* (Orlando: Academic Press, 1984), p. 237.

31. Douglas S. Lipton and Harry K. Wexler, "Breaking the Drug-Crime Connection--Rehabilitation Projects Show Promise," *Corrections Today* 50 (August, 1988): 144, 146, and 155.

32. D. A. Andrews, Ivan Zinger, Robert D. Hoge, James Bonta, Paul Gendreau, and Francis T. Cullen, "Does Correctional Treatment Work? A Clinically Relevant and Psychologically Informed Meta-Analysis," *Criminology* 28 (August, 1990): 369-404.

33. Morris, *The Future of Imprisonment*, p. 26.

34. John P. Conrad, *Justice and Consequences* (Lexington: Lexington Books, 1981), p. 65.

35. Johnson, *Hard Time* p. 162.

36. Nelmes, "The Front Line," p. 46.

37. Ibid.

Chapter 9
DISRUPTIVE AND DISTURBED INMATES

1.   Hans Toch and Kenneth Adams, *Coping: Maladaption in Prisons* (New Brunswick: Transaction, 1989), p. 123.

2.   Ibid., pp. 119-127.

3.   Ibid., pp. 139-151.

4.   Glenn D. Walters, Millard F. Mann, Melvin P. Miller, Leslie L. Hemphill, and Michael L. Chlumsky, "Emotional Disorder among Offenders: Inter- and Intrasetting Comparisons," *Criminal Justice and Behavior* 15 (December, 1988): 433-453.

5.   Toch and Adams, *Coping*, p. 33.

6.   Ibid., p. 254.

7.   Kevin N. Wright, "The Violent and Victimized in the Male Prison," *Journal of Offender Rehabilitation* 16 (1991): 1-25 and Timothy Flanagan, "Correlates of Institutional Misconduct Among State Prisoners," *Criminology* 21 (1983): 29-39.

8.   Toch and Adams, *Coping*, p. 17.

9.   Edward Zamble, "Behavior and Adaptation in Long-term Prison Inmates--Descriptive Longitudinal Results," *Criminal Justice and Behavior* 19 (December, 1992): 409-425 and Doris Layton MacKenzie and Lynne Goodstein, "Long-term Incarceration Impacts and Characteristics of Long-term Offenders--An Empirical Analysis," *Criminal Justice and Behavior* 12 (December, 1985): 395-414.

10. Hans Toch and Kenneth Adams, "Pathology and Disruptiveness Among Prison Inmates," *Journal of Research in Crime and Delinquency* 23 (February, 1986): 7-21.

11. Toch and Adams, *Coping*, pp. 74-75.

12. Ibid., p. 257.

13. H. R. "Hank" Cellini, "The Management and Treatment of Institutionalized Violent Aggressors," *Federal Probation* 50 (Sept. 1986): 51-54.

14. Toch and Adams, *Coping*, p. 261.

15. Ibid.

PART FOUR
LOOKING TOWARD THE FUTURE

1. William G. McGowan, "Information Age Technology--The Competitive Advantage," in *Views From the Top*, ed. Jerome M. Rosow (New York: Facts on File Publications, 1985), p. 131.

2. Kevin Barham and Clive Rssam, *Shaping the Corporate Future--Leading Executives Share Their Vison and Strategies* (London: Unwin Hyman, 1989), p. 112.

3. Harold J. Leavitt, *Corporate Pathfinders: Building Vision and Values into Organizations* (Homewood, IL: Dow Jones-Irwin, 1986), p. 3.

4. Ibid., p. 61.

Chapter 10
DEVELOPING A VISION

1. David C. Evans, "Leadership and Vision in a World of Change," *Corrections Today* 50 (June, 1988): 6.

2. Burt Nanus, "Futures-Creative Leadership," *The Futurist* (May-June, 1990): 14.

3. Kouzes and Posner, *The Leadership Challenge*, p. 87.

4. Ibid., pp. 85-91.

5. Ibid., p. 85.

6. Ibid., pp. 86-87.

7. Leavitt, *Corporate Pathfinders*, pp. 63-66.

8. John W. Gardner, "Leadership and the Future," *The Futurist* (May-June, 1990): 9-12.

9. See Peters, *Thriving on Chaos*, p. 491; Kouzes and Posner, *The Leadership Challenge*, pp. 96-99 and 101-102; Leavitt, *Corporate Pathfinders*, p. 64.

10. Peters, *Thriving on Chaos*, p. 491.

11. Ibid.

12. The idea of a lawful prison was suggest by Conrad, *Justice and Consequence*, pp. 56-59.

13. Gardner, "Leadership," p. 11.

14. Warren Bennis and Burt Nanus, *Leaders* (New York: Harper & Row, 1985), p. 21.

15. Margaret Hambrick, "The Correctional Worker Concept--Being Connected in the 90s," *Federal Prisons Journal* 2 (Winter, 1992): 12.

Chapter 11
STRATEGIC PLANNING

1. Quoted by John M. Bryson, *Strategic Planning for Public and Nonprofit Organizations: A Guide to Strengthening and Sustaining Organizational Achievement* (San Francisco: Jossey Bass, 1989), p. 163.

2. Ibid., p. 32.

3. Bryson, *Strategic Planning*, pp. 32 and xii.

4. Ibid., pp. 48-62. Bryson identified and discussed the seven elements. He included an eighth element, "establishing an effective organizational vision for the future," which I incorporated into clarifying the organizational mission.

5. Ibid., p. 105.

6. *Federal Prisons Journal* 3 (Spring 1992): inside cover.

7. *Federal Prisons Journal* 3 (Spring 1992): inside cover.

8. Elizabeth Kolbert, "Criminal Justice: Elusive Priority in the Cuomo Years," *New York Times*, October 2, 1990, B1 & B5.

9. Bryson, *Strategic Planning*, pp. 139-140 and 56.

10. Ibid., pp. 225-230.

Chapter 12
LEADING INTO THE 21st CENTURY

1.   David W. Helman, "Developing Managers: The Bureau of Prisons' Leadership Forum," *Federal Prisons Journal* 2 (Winter, 1992): 48.

2.   Gardner, *On Leadership*, p. 191.

3.   Ibid., p. 121.

4.   Ibid., pp. 188-189.

5.   Ibid., pp. 124-125 and 188-189.

6.   Ibid., pp. 126-132.

INDEX